Book of Mormon Observations

Volume One

Philip M. Hudson

It is rumored
that there is a certain
Eastern European village
where there still survives a time-
honored tradition. On the first day of
school, the rabbi gives each child a slate
on which the first two letters of the Hebrew
alphabet are written in honey. The child is
then asked to lick up the letters with their
tongue, savor the taste, and to then to use
the slate to learn to read and write, while
remembering how sweet the experience
can be, as long as the endeavor has
been initiated with "a perfect heart
and with a willing mind."
(See 1 Chronicles
28:9).

The great gathering that has
been prophesied in the scriptures (see 3
Nephi Chapter 29 & Ephesians 1:10) is taking
place in our own day, not only among the Jews
in Israel, but also amongst the literal and adopted
descendants of Ephraim, who've been assembling since
1830 to the congregations of The Church of Jesus Christ
of Latter-day Saints. They have been commissioned by
God to bring the message of salvation to a world that
is in desperate need. With priesthood authority and
by the administration of ordinances, Ephraim
will provide the nations of the earth with
the covenant blessings that have been
promised to Abraham and to
his righteous seed.

Copyright 2024 by Philip M. Hudson.
Published 2024.
Printed in the United States of America.
All rights reserved.

No portion of this book may be reproduced,
stored in a retrieval system, or transmitted
in any form or by any means, mechanical,
electronic, photocopy, recording, scanning,
or other, except for brief quotations in
critical reviews or articles, without
the prior written permission
of the author.

ISBN 978-1-957077-66-6
Illustrations - Google Images.

This book may be ordered from
online bookstores.

Publishing Services
by BookCrafters, Parker, Colorado.
www.bookcrafters.net

The
Holy Ghost instills
within each one of us a
sound understanding as we
study The Book of Mormon, that
we might recognize the word of God.
But this is not all; as we give ourselves
to fasting and prayer, we enjoy the spirit
of prophecy and the spirit of revelation, so
that our investigation reveals to our view
the glory, might, majesty, power, and
dominion of God. (See Alma
5:50).

The Nephites were
the happiest when they
observed the summons to
gather in their sanctuaries
to enjoy the companionship
of the Spirit, where they would
receive not only health in their
navels, but also life sustaining
marrow in their bones; even as
their delighted congregations
reverberated with the pleasant
sounds of the anticipation of
an even more enthralling
reunification in heaven
with their Father
Who is their
God.

Table of Contents

Preface..1

Introduction..9

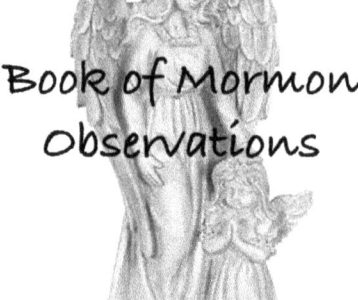

Book of Mormon Observations..13

Also By The Author..297

The children of our Heavenly Father "are instructed sufficiently that they know good from evil." (2 Nephi 2:5). To ensure that our lives are animated with energy, we are blessed with the Light of Christ, proceeding from God's throne as a powerful influence for good that is intended to groom us to receive the Holy Ghost.

The Light of Christ stimulates soul-sweat as it works on our sense of duty and upon our scruples, providing a shield of protection against the corrosive spatter of perspiration that is cast off by the destroyer, who is insidiously and persistently working overtime to damage our doctrinal defenses, dull our spiritual sensitivities, diminish our charitable capacity, deplete our bountiful reservoirs of sympathy, and destroy our devotions, even as we labor with an equal but opposite intensity to deify our work on the earth.

You will quickly see that the
observations expressed on each page in this
volume have been carefully crafted to represent a
variety of geometrical designs. It may be surprising to
learn that the construction of these patterns has helped me to
coherently organize my thoughts. In many cases, the outcome
almost seems to have been foreordained, as I moved words around
until, as if my magic, they dropped into their proper positions on the
page. Often, I had envisioned beforehand the particular framework that I
wanted to achieve, and when I had appropriately arranged the words, one
or two would stand out and grab my attention, because they still didn't
feel quite right. Frequently, it was not difficult to find an alternative
that would not only fit better physically, but also was etymologically
much better suited to the spiritual concept that I wished to convey.
As my work on the project continued, I was intrigued by the
natural evolution of the process. That made me consider
whether my success might have been stimulated
by unconventional thought processes that
are more commonly characterized as
inspiration or discernment.

As you peruse the pages of this book, you will recognize that it is really nothing more than a calendar of sorts, whose observations relate to The Book of Mormon. I wanted to provide a full year's worth of thoughts, which in hindsight turned out to be an ambitious and unrealistic goal. I leave for you, dear reader, to do with these entries what you will. As for me, I can breathe a deep sigh of relief that this endeavor is over, and move on to other writing projects!

You will quickly see that the thoughts that are expressed on each page have been carefully crafted to represent a variety of geometrical designs. It may be surprising to learn that the construction of these patterns has helped me to coherently organize my thoughts. In many cases, the outcome almost seems to have been foreordained, as I moved words around until, as if my magic, they dropped into their proper positions on the page.

Often, I envisioned beforehand the particular framework that I wanted to achieve, and when I had appropriately arranged the words, one or two would stand out and grab my attention, because they still didn't feel quite right. Frequently, it was not difficult to find an alternative that would not only fit better physically, but also was etymologically better suited to the spiritual concept I wished to convey. As my work on the project continued, I was intrigued by the natural evolution of the process. That made me consider whether my success might have been stimulated by unconventional thought processes, that are more commonly characterized as inspiration or discernment.

The various shapes and sizes of the observations on each page reminded me of what vibrant colors must look like to a dog. As I pondered the geometry of the designs that were spread out before me, I realized that they might be manifestations of non-linear thinking in a cynical world that is largely governed by conventional wisdom. Maybe my idiosyncratic ramblings were just an exhibition of thoughts that had taken me down a different path. Maybe I wasn't crazy, or delusional, after all. Perhaps I had been simply touched by the Spirit to think more like a dog.

We will describe non-linear thinking shortly, and in greater detail, but in the meantime, let me tease you with this possibility. Maybe Joseph Smith was one of the first non-linear thinkers. His unconventional view of the world helps to explain why he would look back on his life, and muse: "I stood alone, an unlearned youth, to combat the worldly wisdom and multiplied ignorance of eighteen centuries with a new revelation, which … would open the eyes of more than eight hundred millions of people, and make plain the old paths." (H.C. 6:74). Or: "When we understand the character of God, He begins to unfold the heavens to us, and to tell us all about it. When we are ready to come to Him, He is ready to come to us." (H.C. 6:308). Or, "It is my meditation all the day, and more than my meat and drink, to know how I shall make the Saints of God comprehend the visions that roll like an overflowing surge before my mind. Oh! How I would delight to bring before you things which you never thought of." (H.C. 5:362). Or, "The best way to obtain truth and wisdom is not to ask it from books, but to go to God in prayer, and obtain divine teaching." ("Teachings," p. 191).

Now let us turn to linear thinking, that has been defined as a process of thought following known cycles or step-by-step progression, where a response to any given step must be elicited before another one is taken. This is the conventional way most of us think, most of the time, and in most situations it actually works quite well. However, there is always the danger of relying too heavily on the sheer logic of linear thinking for once we have settled upon a starting point in our inquiry, there are only a limited number of avenues that lead to logical conclusions. Additionally, there is no guarantee that our starting point relies on truth, or on what I would call eternally valid principles. If we are lucky, and it does, we are certainly going to be much better off than if we had chosen a starting point that was either blatantly false, or that was so narrowly defined that it would limit our exposure to the rich variety of alternatives that might just be the best ones to provide the answers to our inquiry.

Linear thinking is a
process of thought following
a known cycle or a step-by-step
progression, where a response to a step
must be elicited before another one is taken.
This is the conventional way most of us think,
most of the time, and in most situations it actually
works quite well. However, there is always the possibility of
relying too heavily on the sheer logic of linear thinking, for once
we have settled upon a starting point in our inquiry, there are only a
limited number of options that lead to logical conclusions. Additionally,
there is no guarantee that our starting point relies on truth, or on eternally
valid principles. If we are lucky, and it does, we are certainly going to be much
better off than if we had chosen a starting point that was either blatantly false, or
that was so narrowly defined that it would limit our exposure to a rich variety of
alternatives that might be the best ones to provide the answers to our inquiry.
In any event, we risk being led astray right from the beginning, and
then finding ourselves in unfamiliar, indefensible territory from
which there is no easy avenue of escape. Linear thinking is
dangerous if it takes us down the road of expediency
that leads to ethical and moral dilemmas,
and to conundrums that can be
of cosmic proportions.

In any event, we risk being led astray right from the beginning, and then finding ourselves in unfamiliar, indefensible territory from which there is no easy avenue of escape. Linear thinking is dangerous when it takes us down the road of expediency that leads to ethical and moral dilemmas, and to conundrums that can be of cosmic proportions.

Non-linear thinking, as opposed to linear thinking, is a relatively new term, which means that there is a lot of obfuscation going on when attempting to articulate its definition. But, for the sake of simplicity, let's describe it as human thought that is characterized by cerebral expansion in multiple spatial and even temporal directions, rather than in just one pre-determined linear direction. It is based on the concept that there exist multiple starting points from which the basic principles of logical thought may be applied to a problem. Consider, once again, my characterization of Joseph Smith as one of the most celebrated (and misunderstood and maligned) non-linear thinker of the Nineteenth Century.

We do not have to stretch our minds very much to be immediately struck by the realization that God Himself must be the quintessential non-linear thinker, that the Plan of Salvation, with all of its permutations and combinations, is its best expression, and that it might be consistent with His design to view the gospel through the clarifying lens of similar unconventional thought processes.

Non-linear thinking is expansive, and it lets creative juices run wild precisely because it is not dependent upon a narrowly defined self-limiting structure. It increases the sheer number of possible outcomes because it encourages multiple starting points for any train of thought. There is enough room in the world for an infinite number of non-linear thinkers, which allows us to segue right into the basic premises of the Plan of Salvation. The Plan, too, is flexible enough to accommodate those of every persuasion and inclination, for God "inviteth them all to come unto him and partake of his goodness; and he denieth none that come unto him, black and white, bond and free, male and female; and he remembereth the heathen; and all are alike unto God, both Jew and Gentile." (2 Nephi 26:33).

Non-linear thinkers who happen to be lucky enough to consciously appreciate the elasticity of the Plan of Salvation have flexible testimonies. To them, the veil is almost transparent. They are spiritually sensitive and prepared to act upon their own promptings, unconventional though they may be. As their powers expand, they experience the glittering facets of the life of the Spirit. They find themselves cast off into streams of revelation, as if they were being carried along in the quickening currents of direct experience with God. Non-linear thinking sets them free to be creative, and sets them creative, that they might be free to investigate unconventional or previously unexplored options. In a sense, we all enter this world as non-linear thinkers. We are "born free," as it were. If that is true, from the very beginning, the stage was set for the inauguration of the perfect law of liberty. We are nurtured from our birth to master the ability to generate higher-level non-linear thought processes, so that the quiet spiritual stirrings that underlie our experience might be amplified and become the very catalyst we need to propel us into the holy presence of the mind, or the gnosis, of God.

Non-linear thinkers have no privileged frames of reference, which opens up almost unlimited options for them. They jump around, forward and backward, up and down, and side to side, when working through a problem. They literally see the big picture, from a larger perspective, as they move from one point on the canvas of life to another, focusing with greater sensitivity on areas that have caught their attention. This sounds a lot like how we envision God governing His creations.

Think of a linear slide show, contrasted with the comprehension of a huge canvas that illustrates the entire story, not from start to finish, but all at once, the beginning and the end at one and the same time, with the additional capacity

In the thoughts expressed in this book, I hope that I have employed the best techniques of both liner and non-linear thinking, because I believe that ultimately, both are useful and important cognitive devices that we need to master. Non-linear thinking, however, is at its best when we re-examine our potential starting points, because doing that increases the possibility of selecting the best alternative from all those that are available. But somewhere during the process of inquiry, after that critical starting point has been fixed in our crosshairs, we might also want to employ linear thinking because of its efficient logic-based reasoning. Once we have embarked upon the journey, linear thinking might help us to get to the finish line in a more timely manner. How effectively we use both devices depends upon how thoroughly we've read the play book, how vigorously we exercise our gift of free will along the way, and how often we rely upon powers greater than ourselves to make necessary course corrections, in order to re-align ourselves with our envisioned goals and recalibrate our efforts to achieve them.

to zoom in and out, to fast forward, reverse, and freeze frame. If you can visualize that, you can see why God must be a non-linear thinker. With a little practice, we can be, too.

In the thoughts expressed in this book, I hope that I have employed the best techniques of both liner and non-linear thinking, because I believe that ultimately, both are useful and important cognitive devices to be mastered. Non-linear thinking, however, is at its best when we re-examine our potential starting points, because doing that increases our chances of selecting the right option from all the alternatives available. But somewhere during the process of inquiry, after that critical starting point has been fixed in our crosshairs, we might also want to employ linear thinking because of its efficient logic-based reasoning. Once we have embarked upon the journey, linear thinking might help us to focus our attention and get to the finish line in a more timely manner. How effectively we use both devices depends upon how thoroughly we have read the play book, how vigorously we exercise our gift of free will along the way, and how often we rely upon Powers greater than ourselves to make necessary course corrections, in order to re-align ourselves with Their greater wisdom, better envision goals, and recalibrate our efforts to achieve them.

As you read the Observations in this book, look for examples of both linear and non-linear thinking, and decide for yourself how to best incorporate them into your own style of inquiry.

I don't sit around and make
this stuff up. I really don't. Maybe this preface
is the product of a tumor that causes my brain to fire
unconventionally. I should really check out that possibility;
maybe have an MRI. I know one thing, however: I have learned to
keep my computer by my bedside, and to record the thoughts that
pop into my mind as I fall asleep, or when I wake up with a jolt.
"For God speaketh once, yea twice, yet man perceiveth it not.
In a dream, in a vision of the night, when deep sleep
falleth upon men, in slumberings upon the bed;
Then he openeth the ears of men, and sealeth
their instruction." (Job 33:14-16).

Introduction

All
around
the world, the
gospel is shared by
way of a hierarchy that
is based on understanding
at first, and next on acceptance,
then on commitment, and finally
on recommitment. Preaching is similar
to understanding, teaching to acceptance,
expounding to commitment, and exhortation
to re-commitment. Testimony is an expression of
action that follows the internalization of principles.
It is borne with strenuous effort that reflects the price
that has been paid to understand the voice of the Lord
concerning those principles. Testimony is a reflection
of the value placed on direct experience with the Spirit
as it teaches us about those principles. Testimony is
not free, but is purchased at considerable expense.
Testimony releases the power of principles, their
merit and validity, and empowers us to bind
ourselves to those principles by covenants
of action that increase our strength
and endurance, day by day, as
we learn to rely upon the
Lord in all that we
say and do.

Our faith in
the wise counsel
of Book of Mormon
prophets can vitalize
the moral fiber we
need to face our
demons.

Hugh Nibley observed: "Men fool themselves, when they think for a moment that they can read scripture without ever adding something to the text or omitting something from it." Therein lies the power inherent in its study. We glean insight and understanding every time we investigate the word of God. I have learned to love the scriptures, and I often think of St. Hilary, who wrote: "Scripture consists not in what we read, but in what we understand." In these Observations I have consistently tried to anchor the ideas swirling around in my head to the scriptures.

Reading my Observations as they relate to The Book of Mormon does not replace personal scripture study. The spiritual awakening that accompanies prayerful efforts to understand the mysteries of God through the study of His word cannot be achieved through another person's interpretation. Perhaps, though, my own perspectives on the eternal themes expressed within The Book of Mormon will be helpful to you as you read and seek your own guidance. It is my hope that you will use these compendia only to assist you in your own personal journey to Christ.

Our challenge is to enlist the aid of the Holy Ghost as we undertake that journey. Many years ago, Dallin Oaks observed that Latter-day Saints know that compendia can help us with scriptural interpretation, but they must be used with caution. They "are not substitutes for the scriptures any more than a good cookbook is a substitute for food. When I refer to "commentaries," I mean everything that interprets scripture, from the comprehensive book-length commentary to the brief interpretation embodied in a lesson or an article, such as this one."

"One trouble with commentaries," he continued, "is that their authors sometimes focus on only one meaning to the exclusion of others. As a result, commentaries, if not used with great care, may illuminate the author's chosen and correct meaning but close our eyes and restrict our horizons to other possible meanings. Sometimes, those other less obvious meanings can be the ones most valuable and useful to us as we seek to obtain answers to our own questions. This is why the teaching of the Holy Ghost is a better guide to scriptural interpretation than is even the best commentary." ("Ensign," 1/1985).

Harold B. Lee taught: "We are convinced that our members are hungry for the gospel undiluted, with its abundant truths and insights. There are those who have seemed to forget that the most powerful weapons the Lord has given us against all that is evil are His own declarations - the plain and simple doctrines of salvation as found in the scriptures." (Regional Representatives Seminar, 10/1/1970).

Bruce R. McConkie explained that "revelation is necessary because … each pronouncement in the holy scriptures is so written as to reveal little or much, depending on the spiritual capacity of the student." ("A New Witness for The Articles of Faith," p. 71).

And so, as President Oaks continued, "the scriptures are not the ultimate source of knowledge, but what precedes the ultimate source. The ultimate source comes by revelation. We encourage everyone to make careful study of the scriptures and of prophetic teachings … and to prayerfully seek personal revelation to know their meaning for themselves … If we seek and accept revelation and inspiration to enlarge our understanding, we will have the mysteries of God unfolded to us by the power of the Holy Ghost."

Joseph Smith himself spoke in what he characterized as his own 'crooked, broken, scattered, and imperfect language'. (Joseph Smith to William W. Phelps, 11/27/1832, quoted in "Making Sense of the Doctrine & Covenants, a Guided Tour Through Modern Revelation," Steven Harper. "Personal Writings of Joseph Smith," p. 186-287,). In this Compendium, I are sure that I have come nowhere near matching Joseph's language, so please, dear reader, bear with me, as you work your way through this volume.

Alma the Younger
is a good example of a repentant
sinner who fasted and prayed many
days to receive the spirit of revelation, and
to know and understand the things of God. (See
Alma 5:45-46). As we fast, the spiritual and temporal
sides of our nature slowly harmonize. Our physical desires,
held in check by an expanding spiritual awareness, strengthen
our resolve to discipline our nature. We transcend forces pulling
us one way or the other, and enter a metaphysical state of euphoria
where virtue garnishes our thoughts unceasingly, as the doctrine
of the priesthood distills upon our souls as the dews from heaven
because our confidence begins to wax strong in the presence of
God. As this process unfolds, the Holy Ghost becomes our
constant companion, our scepter an unchanging scepter
of righteousness and truth, and our dominion a God
centered and focused protectorate. Under these
conditions, all that is good begins to freely
flow like an artesian well from the
fountain of heaven, in an
unending stream.

When
a faithless society has
been weighed in the balances
and is found wanting, it can be
traced all the way back to spiritual
bankruptcy on an institutional scale;
simply to its denial of the power of the
doctrine within The Book of Mormon.
Its motto seems to be: 'Eat, drink,
and be merry, for tomorrow we
will surely die.' (See
Luke 12:19).

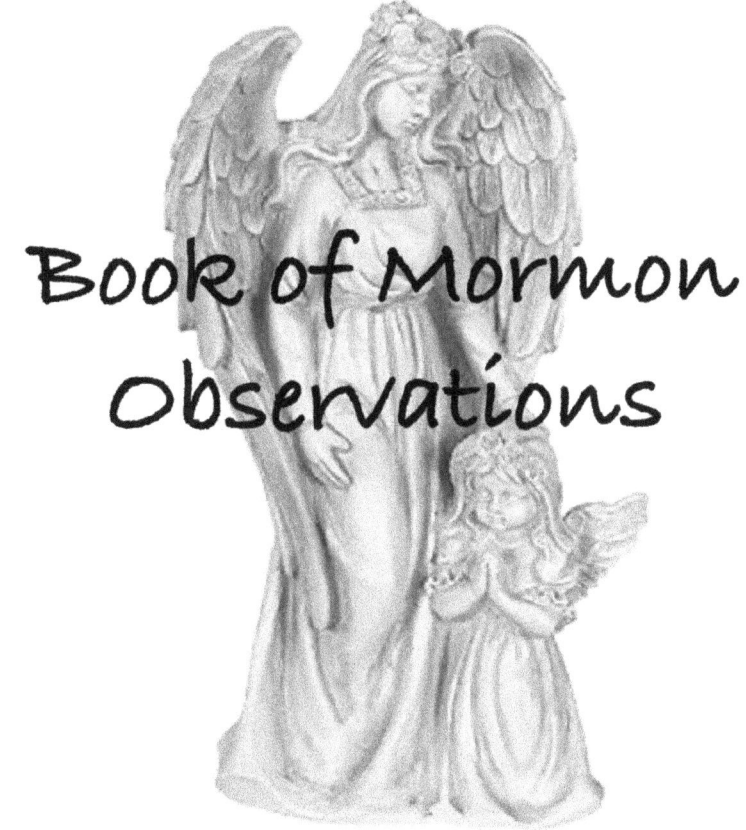

Book of Mormon Observations

Historically, and sadly, organized religion has
become magical in the eyes of the most devout believers
when the power of the church has been transferred from God to
those who profess to be His earthly representatives, but who are,
in reality, only competing for market share. Priesthood acquires
the status of an office that mechanically bestowing both blessings
and grace, regardless of the moral or spiritual qualifications of its
possessor. The Bible then appears to convey power and knowledge
without the need for revelation. Moroni saw that there would be
many in the Last Days, who had "transfigured the holy
word of God," or who had wrested the scriptures, by
changing their appearance and substance
to meet their profane needs.
(Mormon 8:33).

The Book of Mormon emphasizes
that we must never allow ourselves to
squander precious energy by becoming
preoccupied with what is missing. Focusing
our attention on what we lack could become a
paralyzing fear. It's a flawed strategy that will
ultimately defeat us. We must concentrate on
the resources that are available, be they large
or small, capitalize on them, and turn them
into forces for positive, substantive, and
significant change. We must pray as
if everything depended upon the
will of God, as it surely does,
but then work as if it all
depended upon us.

The Book of Mormon teaches that
if we did not have a Redeemer to atone
for our sins, it would be impossible for us
to enjoy celestial glory. In our fallen state
and with no avenue of escape, we would be
left incapable of obedience to the celestial
principles that govern God's kingdom,
and we would live forever in our sins.
Thus, the great Plan of Salvation,
and the purpose of temples,
would be frustrated.

When we are
steadfast in Book of Mormon
scholarship. we enjoy a knowledge
of God's truth and we are of a sound
understanding. We diligently search
the scriptures that we might recognize
His word, and when we fast and pray,
we have the spirit of prophecy and of
revelation, and when we teach, we
we do so with the power and the
authority of God. (See
Alma 17:2-3).

"There is no parallelistic figure of speech that
should become more important than the Book of Mormon's
chief message, which is to convince both "Jew and Gentile that
Jesus is the Christ, the Eternal God" (Book of Mormon Title Page).
Instead, all of these forms and figures are designed to present this
message regarding Jesus Christ and his gospel in an unforgettable,
understandable, artistic, and fascinating way. These forms and
figures gave writers of scripture unique methods of expression
as they set forth religious doctrines, tenets, and principles.
Apparently, the prophets and writers of the scriptures
employed the repetition of alternating parallel
lines for the purpose of reinforcing their
teachings and doctrines." (Donald
W. Parry, "Poetic Parallelisms in
The Book of Mormon").

For those who are adventurous
enough to tackle reading the entire Book of
Mormon with its multitudinous parallelisms
comprehensively documented and annotated in a
readable fashion, I highly recommend the following
scholarly work: "Poetic Parallelisms in The Book
of Mormon," Donald W. Parry, Brigham Young
University, BYU Scholars Archive, Maxwell
Institute Publications, 2007.

The Book of
Mormon blesses
us with easy fluency
in a heavenly language
that is rhythmical, melodious,
soothing to our ears, and calming
to our souls. When we hear the Spirit
quietly whisper: "You're a stranger here,"
we are comforted by the realization that
we have "wandered from a more
exalted sphere." (Eliza
R. Snow).

It is our belief that may
sanction the truthfulness of a
precept, principle, or doctrine, but
it often does so without the moral
element of responsibility which we
call faith. Of those to whom much is
given, though, much is expected. The
gift of faith to believe in The Book of
Mormon demands action. So, when
we exercise our agency, even if we've
performed good works, if we do so
without an abiding trust in the
promise of Moroni with which
we have all been blessed, our
works will fall short of
the mark, because
our faith lacks
vitality.

It makes very little difference to
Heavenly Father whether we are combating
the temptations of the Seven Deadly Sins, or
simply the garden-variety transgressions that
plague us all. The teachings of the prophets in
The Book of Mormon stipulate that we must go
thru a process of repentance before we can be
admitted into the Church of Jesus Christ
through baptism, and receive the
gifts of the Spirit.

Our own
journey to the veil
recalls the wisdom of
Winston Churchill, who
said: "There comes for each
of us a special moment when
we are figuratively tapped on the
shoulder and offered a chance to do a
very special thing, unique to ourselves
and fitted to our talents. What a tragedy
if that moment should find us unprepared
or unqualified for that which could have been
our finest hour." Standing before God, angels,
and witnesses at the Judgment Bar, it will be a
fitting conclusion to the hours that have been
spent as eager participants in a preparatory
excursion through The Book of Mormon.

Thomas Jefferson wrote about "The religion builders" of his day who "had so distorted and deformed the doctrines of Jesus, so muffled them in mysticisms, fancies and falsehoods, and had caricatured them into forms so inconceivable, as to shock reasonable thinkers. Happy in the prospect of a restoration of primitive Christianity, I must leave it to younger persons," he concluded, "to encounter and lop off the false branches which have been grafted into it by the mythologists of the middle and modern ages."

There is no revelation where there is no student, and so as long as we ask the wrong questions relating to The Book of Mormon, we will be at odds with faith. Our rational minds will never be able to bridge the gap that must exist between the profane character of the worldly-wise and the wisdom manifested in God's divine nature.

The account of
God's Creation that
has survived in the Bible
provides precious few details
that relate to the Fall of Adam
and Eve and to the Atonement of
Christ, which is the doctrine that we
must understand in order to have the
faith to be clean from the blood and
sins of our generation, live life in
abundance, and become heirs of
salvation. Fortunately, these
doctrines are explained with
stunning clarity in The
Book of Mormon.

Every time that
we drag ourselves to the
mercy seat of the Savior and
prostrate ourselves upon the altar
of faith, gratitude swells in our hearts,
and we marvel how The Book of Mormon
has lifted our spirits. We examine our lives
through the magnifying lens of the Spirit
to look for ways to improve. Because of our
repentance, the Savior becomes the wind
beneath our wings, and because of
Him, we find ourselves soaring
higher than the eagles.

Every time we
encounter the principles
of the Plan during our study
of The Book of Mormon, we find the
sinews of our bodies resonating with
religious recognition as we have our
déjà vu moments. At the end of the
day, every one who hearkens to
the voice of the Spirit will
eventually come unto
God in this way,
and really
live.

It is in
The Book of Mormon
where we learn about the
autobiographical thread that
is intertwined with our sinews,
that winds its way to our Father
in Heaven. The Holy Ghost helps
us to remember the lesson that has
been stitched into our souls: That
we have been placed on the earth
for one reason alone – that it
might become a machine
for the making of
gods.

Consistent with the book of Psalms (149:1), wherein ancient Israel was described as "a congregation of Saints," and on 30 other occasions in the Old Testament, and at least 73 cases in the New Testament, where the members of the church were characterized as "saints," in The Book of Mormon, both Jacob and Benjamin employed that term to describe the righteous who believed in the Holy One of Israel. (See 2 Nephi 9:18 & Mosiah 3:19).

There will come an "a ha!" moment for those who continue to wrestle to embrace The Book of Mormon, when the sun shall not go down, "neither shall the moon withdraw itself. For the Lord shall be their everlasting light." (Isaiah 60:20).

Saving faith has to be more than just an intellectual acknowledgement of the gospel principles that are championed in The Book of Mormon. As a vital contrary, its influence will extend only as far as our deeds. Therefore, our works become a necessary companion to our vital, active confidence that the power of the Word will have enough inherent energy to guide us through the transformation of our lives into new creatures in Christ.

The elements of our Father's Plan that are clearly defined in The Book of Mormon speak to our spirits, for every principle of the gospel carries within itself a witness that it is true. Its language is universal and when our minds have been illuminated by faith, we enjoy familiarity, fluency, and an easy comfort with the revealed word of God that opens up vistas of eternal proportion before our eyes.

As the Holy Ghost guides us to embrace the creative expressions within The Book of Mormon, we begin to understand how their energy helps us to appreciate God. We begin to feel the divine potential within us, and we are charged with the confidence to ask seemingly simple questions that can have profound answers and implications that shake our world, spreading like the ripples radiating outward from a rock thrown into the still water of our perceptual ponds. We begin to see the book for what it really is, and that is as a revelatory machine for the making of Gods.

Babylon's image consultants are prone to confuse conventional wisdom with the weightier matters of the law in the tumultuous last days on earth. Mormon cautioned: "Take heed, that ye do not judge that which is evil to be of God, or that which is good and of God to be of the devil." (Moroni 7:14). In the vast arena that is the world, there are no shades of gray for those who have not only received the Light of Christ, but also the greater power of the Holy Ghost. For to them it is given "to judge, that (they) may know good from evil; and the way to judge is as plain, that ye may know with a perfect knowledge, as the daylight is from the dark night." (Moroni 7:15).

The Book of
Mormon catalyzes
our tenacity to bear our
testimonies to the world, of
what we have been taught by
the Spirit, and to certify that
it has been as profound for us
as it was for the multitude on
the Day of Pentecost, when the
witness of Peter and the other
apostles carried the day as it
penetrated the hearts of all
who heard them, giving
them the desire to ask:
"What must we do if
we want to inherit
eternal life?"

The virtues that
we acknowledge as the
tender mercies of God (see 1
Nephi 1:20) focus on their ability
to touch our hearts and change our
nature, to soften us, and to humble
us, to make us as pliant clay in the
hands of the Master Potter, to mold
us as children, and to securely
envelop our spirits within the
vale of happiness that has
has been prepared for
the Saints.

To the
people among
whom Alma the
Younger ministered,
it may have seemed that
the easier wrong was more
expedient, but that was because
it harmonized with the values of
Babylon. Worldliness surrounded
the Nephites throughout all the land,
and without the stabilizing influence
of the word of God to choose the harder
right, moral equivocation had become
the easier way out, defining bad
bad habit patterns of behavior
that required his timely
intervention.

Alma showed
his Nephite brethren
how to generate sufficient
faith to burst free of their self-
imposed limitations, teaching how
God has ordained a Plan whereby we
might one day attain His stature and
become all that He now is. But we may do
this only if we've incorporated into our being
and nature His image and likeness. Through
that transformative process, Alma taught that
our corruption will take on incorruption, and
our bodies will become clean, pure, and
will stream with intrinsic light.

Nephi, the son of Helaman, believed that gaining a testimony of the gospel would require that his people prostrate themselves before the mercy seat of the Lord, that they might more easily feel the sweet influence of the Spirit. He understood that without such a token of contrition, God's "wisdom cannot reveal itself, culture cannot become manifest, strength cannot fight, wealth becomes useless, and intelligence cannot be applied." (Heraclitus, ancient Greek philosopher, from Ephesus).

Alma had taught his grandson Nephi a wonderful truth, that, in the resurrection, we will inherit glorified bodies and we will become re-acquainted with our spirits, never again to be separated by sin. In fact, Alma taught that "the spirit and the body shall be reunited again in its perfect form; both limb and joint shall be restored to its proper frame." (Alma 11:43). Therefore, it makes sense that we would want to keep our bodies as pure and as holy as are our spirits, in order for the gospel to bless our lives, starting right now, as was envisioned by the Plan of our Father in Heaven.

The
direct frontal
assault by he who
is the adversary of all
that's good and of the godly
principles that are espoused by
The Book of Mormon, utilizes the
mutated forms of honor, truth, love,
generosity, and virtue. These dreadful
distortions of character are made up of
bellicose behaviors, recalcitrant rituals,
cunning customs, treacherous telestial
traditions, hostile habits, duplicitous
deviations, insincere institutions,
and sneaky social conventions.
These fiery contrarian darts
have the power to sabotage
our noblest intentions
to embrace the
truth.

Book of Mormon
prophet-historians provide
unequivocal understanding
and unambiguous definitions of
eternal truth. They allow us to benefit
from the events within which we are swept
up, to learn from our relationships with others,
to grow within our environment no matter how
unique or difficult it might seem to us, and
to protect ourselves from worldly influences
that would encroach upon the fortress of
our spiritual security, symmetry,
and sanctuary.

If it were possible to
bring together all the written
records from our past, we would find
that, overwhelmingly, they are "religious
in nature; that the primary purpose to which
writing has been put thru the ages has been for
keeping a remembrance of God's dealing with
men." (Hugh Nibley). A striking exception to
this rule has been the profusion of the profane
propaganda that has poured from the press
like an avalanche, in the past 200 years.
Satan's secular humanists have at last
found their forum for falsehood in both
the print and electronic media. Little
wonder that Jacob warned us that to
be learned is good, but only if we
hearken to the counsel of God.
(See 2 Nephi 9:29).

The
blessing of
doctrine that is
found in The Book
of Mormon is within
the reach of all of us, no
matter what our cultural,
social, political, economic,
or religious proclivities may
be. The principles that testify
of its universal applicability
and accessibility are bolstered
by the avowal of our Heavenly
Father that He is no respecter
of persons. (See Acts
10:34).

Among the Nephites, their outward observances of the Law were as phylacteries. (See 2 Nephi 25:27-30). In The Book of Mormon, we repeatedly see that real justification only comes thru saving faith in the principles and ordinances of the gospel. Really, there are only 2 ways that lie before us. "One leads to an ever lower and lower plane, where are heard cries of despair and the curses of the poor, where manhood shrivels and possessions wear down the bearer; while the other leads to the highlands of the morning, where are heard the glad shouts of humanity, and where honest effort is rewarded with immortality." (John Altgeld).

Those who are stiff-necked have skin so thick and calloused that extraordinary means become necessary to penetrate and touch theirs spirit. Enos reported: "There was nothing save it was exceeding harshness, preaching, and prophesying of wars, and contentions, and destructions, and continually reminding them of death, and the duration of eternity, and the judgments and the power of God, and all these things, stirring them up continually to keep them in the fear of the Lord. I say there was nothing short of these things, and exceedingly great plainness of speech, would keep them from going down speedily to destruction." (Enos 1:23).

The effort that we've put into making
the teachings of The Book of Mormon a part
of our lives will leave the world a better place than
when we found it. When we pass beyond the veil, we
will leave our loved ones with a legacy of both tangible
and intangible remembrance. We will leave them with
testimony. We will leave them with gratitude for the
privilege and blessing to have been knit together
as a family that is both the corporeal footing
and the incorporeal foundation of our
Heavenly Father's great Plan
of Happiness.

The prophets
have blessed us with
the eternal truths of the
gospel, and they do so in
plainness and simplicity, so
that all might understand. It is
the nature of the apostolic calling
to bear witness to all of the world of
the divinity of Jesus Christ and teach
the path to salvation and exaltation in
ways that are easily understood. Since
the Bible is today ambiguous, unclear,
and even contradictory, it must be the
result of errors of both omission and
commission that were introduced
by uninspired, untutored, and
even malicious copyists
over the years. (See 1
Nephi 13:28).

For
the Nephites,
the gospel was the
perfect law of liberty,
setting them free to make
good decisions, free to receive
the blessings of the priesthood,
and free to serve others in more
powerful and significant ways.
They were free to enjoy unlimited
opportunity for improvement as
they committed themselves to
the principles of the Plan of
Salvation. They were free
to improve their lives,
beginning in time,
but continuing
in eternity.

Despite
an abundance
of gold and silver
throughout the land,
all the Nephites really
had to show for themselves
was their character, and each
one of them told their own story.
Theirs was a record that couldn't lie
inasmuch as it was written within the
sinews of their bodies, as well as upon the
fleshy tables of their hearts. Theirs was a
chronicle that will one day be unfolded
before God, angels, and witnesses, who
will innocently ask if they wouldn't
mind providing the narrative.

If we are startled by
the corruptible reflection
that we see as we pass by the
windows of a great and spacious
building (see 1 Nephi 8:31 & 11:36),
we'll need to repent without hesitation,
remembering that "the Lord seeth not
as man seeth; for man looketh on
the outward appearance, but the
Lord looketh on the heart."
(1 Samuel 16:7).

The Prophet Alma often
spoke of being "born again." Of the
people in the land of Mormon, he said:
"Behold, (Jesus Christ) changed their hearts;
yea, he awakened them out of a deep sleep, and
they awoke unto God. Behold, they were in the midst
of darkness; nevertheless, their souls were illuminated
by the light of the everlasting word." (Alma 5:7, see Alma
7:14, 22:15, & 36:24). Those who have been born again leave
behind their former lives, and become alive to the things of the
Spirit. They promise to never again return to their wicked ways.
They change their names and become "saints, a translation of
a Greek word that is also rendered 'holy,' the fundamental
idea being that of consecration or separation for a sacred
purpose; but since what was set apart for God must
be without blemish, the word came to mean 'free
from blemish,' whether physical or moral. In
the New Testament, the saints are those
who by baptism have entered into
the Christian covenant."
("Bible Dictionary").

It is a characteristic of the Last Days that society has become increasingly polarized. On the one hand we see the kingdom of God, and on the other is the kingdom of the devil. Satan's kingdom is typified as a corrupt or idolatrous community. There are, after all, "save two churches only; the one is the church of the Lamb of God, and the other is the church of the devil' wherefore, whoso belongeth not to the church of the Lamb of God belongeth to that great church, which is the mother of abominations; and she is the whore of all the earth."
(1 Nephi 14:10).

With trepidation, we acknowledge that The Book of Mormon has become a blueprint for survival in the Last Days. Ours was to have been an Age of Enlightenment, but it has become a conceptual free-for-all, without rules, regulations, or constraints of any kind. Righteousness has always responded to the better angels of our nature because it reflects foundation principles that are not subject to the vagaries of men. While man may cope with the trauma of secular humanism, he cannot live for long with unrighteousness before it strangles his spontaneity as an evolving child of God.

The Adversary of all that is good knows all the tricks and his strategies among the Nephites and Lamanites were not so very different from those that he employs today. He advocates evil by making drinking and smoking look 'cool', and by rationalizing cheating, lying, and even stealing. He plays mind games with us to get us to use drugs, and he clothes the latest fashions in fine twined linens. Immorality and swearing are woven into popular music and hit movies. He minimizes the seriousness of sin by telling us "Everyone's doing it." "It doesn't hurt anyone else." "Just once won't hurt." "I can always repent later." It's not a big deal." And even, "The devil made me do it."

The prophets speak to us out of the pages of The Book of Mormon, inviting us to be baptized, that we might enjoy the quiet serenity of the Sabbath day as we never have before. We are introduced to new experiences during our day of worship, service, and rest that take us far from the tumult of the teeming multitudes and the telestial crowd that too often reflects the lifestyle of the rich and famous.

The wicked Lamanites felt
neither love nor loyalty for anything
or anyone else but themselves, and enjoyed
neither the blessings of unity nor the peace that
was the province solely of the righteous. Instead, the
father of contention, who is Satan, oversaw their self-
destruction and he perversely enjoyed the process. They
were punished by their sins, and not so much for them.
We think that it is God Who applies punishment, and
that He does it externally, the way parents often do,
but He does not. We say "If you don't clean your
room, you can't drive the car for a week." God
God says, "If you don't clean your room,
you'll have to live in it for a week."
As it turns out, each of us has
to endure the consequences
of our disobedience
to eternal law.

When the hearts of the
wicked are hardened against the
admonitions of The Book of Mormon
and minds are closed to its message of
salvation, light is diminished, leaving their
faltering spirits vulnerable to the relentlessly
aggressive tactics of the Devil. Left alone, they are
influenced more by the lies of the Deceiver than by
illuminating truth, and they risk being dragged
by the heavy weight of his chains of darkness
down to the hell of misunderstanding,
ignorance, and self-destructive
patterns of behavior.

The Cedars of Lebanon
that are spoken of in the scriptures
were evergreen, beautiful, aromatic, wide
2 Nephi 12:13 & 24:8). Members of the church are
represented as cedars of Lebanon. They will declare that
since the destruction of Babylon, no feller, a person who
cuts down trees, has come up against them to smite them.
In similar manner, it's the righteous who shall "flourish
like the palm tree (and) grow like a cedar in Lebanon.
Those that (are) planted in the house of the Lord shall
flourish in the courts of our God." (Psalms 92:12).
Cedars of Lebanon may grow in what appear to
be harsh environments. It is only upon closer
inspection that the oasis of an underlying
current of life-sustaining water may be
noticed, that brings nourishment
to the roots of the thirsty trees.

"I believe our state after death
will be beautiful with colour, music,
and speech of flowers and faces I love. (See
Moroni 10:34). Without this faith, there would be
little meaning in my life. I should be a mere pillar
of darkness in the dark. Observers in the full enjoyment
of their bodily senses pity me, but it is because they do not see
the golden chamber in my life where I dwell delighted; for dark as
my path may seem to be, I carry a magic light in my heart. Faith,
the spiritual strong searchlight, illuminates the way, and although
sinister doubts lurk in the shadow, I walk unafraid towards the
Enchanted Wood where the foliage is always green, where joy
abides, where nightingales nest and sing, and where life
and death are one in the presence of the Lord."
(Helen Keller, "Midstream").

The Book
of Mormon speaks
"of things as they really are,
and of things as they really will
be," which are manifest in plainness
for the salvation of our souls. (Jacob 4:13).
In contrast is the intellectual embroidery that
is at times preferred to the whole ensemble of
the gospel; the frills to the fabric, as it were.
The Book of Mormon gives us the absolute
anchors that we so desperately need. If
we give it a chance, we will find that
there is more realism in the word
of God than there could ever
be in a secularism that is
congenitally short
sighted.

The
Book of
Mormon fans
with our faith the
fires of our resolve.
We hope and pray to
have courage to change
the things we can, for the
serenity to accept the things
we cannot, and for God's
wisdom to know the
difference.

The
Book
of Mormon
endows us with
the strength to watch
ourselves judiciously, to
be the meticulous guardians
of our thoughts, the scrupulous
custodians of our words, and the
prudent caretakers of our deeds, to
fastidiously observe all of the
commandments of God by
continuing evenly in
the faith.

Nephi
exhorted you and
me to put on the armour
of God, and to press forward
with dedication, steadfastness,
confidence, and a firm determination
in Christ, with a perfect brightness of hope,
or perfect faith, and charity, or a love of God
and of all men. When we do not just casually
sample the words of Christ, but feast upon them,
enduring in righteousness through this veil of
tears to the very end, we will have eternal
life, which is the greatest gift that
can be bestowed upon us by
our Heavenly Father.

We can be
fully converted to
the gospel, and even
have a testimony of The
Book of Mormon, but still
enjoy very special moments
of reconfirmation. The Spirit
sometimes works so powerfully
upon us that we can say that our
hearts have been changed through
faith on the name of Christ, that
we have been born of Him, and
that we have become His sons
and daughters. We no longer
have the disposition to do
evil, but to do good
continually.

We are
converted to
the doctrine of
Christ in 2 Nephi
Chapter 31, as it calls
to us, bidding us to come
in out of the cold; out of the
darkness into the light of day.
We are the acorns of a mighty
oak. Our testimony of Christ
inspires us to reconnect
with our intrinsic
nobility.

The Book of Mormon illustrates that even the righteous do not become perfect overnight. Therefore, the Lord has promised that as often as we repent, He will forgive us our trespasses. He will give us enough rope to either hang ourselves, or to lasso the stars and hitch our wagons to eternity. The choice is ours to make.

Faith, light, and truth may be recognized as irreducible common denominators. They are the essential elements of an equation that describes the foundation upon which a testimony of The Book of Mormon is based. "One for all and all for one!" was the motto of the Three Musketeers. Without faith, light, and truth, said Joseph Smith, we would "degenerate from God, descend to the devil, and lose knowledge," and without it, we cannot become converted to the gospel.

Each time we "press forward with a steadfastness in Christ, having a perfect brightness of hope, and a love of God and of all men," we are "feasting upon" His words and hear His voice. Our experience is then validated by an unimpeachable witness and a spiritual re-confirmation that we receive from the Holy Ghost.
(2 Nephi 31:20).

Christianity enjoys prominence as the most universally recognized religion in history, comprising a majority of the population in 2/3 of the world's 196 countries. Almost 2 billion people, 31% of the world's citizens, claim membership in 33,820 identifiable denominations. Islam is next with 1.2 billion people, and there are 14 million Jews. (Source: World Christian Encyclopedia). The intention of The Book of Mormon is not to detract from the devotion to correct principles of any Christians or non-Christians among whom they teach and testify. Those who are receptive to the messages of the Restoration are encouraged to keep what the Spirit has already taught them to be true. The only purpose of proselytizing is so that "faith might also increase in the earth, "and that the Lord's everlasting' covenant might be established."
(D&C 1:21-22).

Certainly, our finest hours are
those when our unexpected challenges
have been met with extraordinary effort.
Just like the Seven Dwarfs, when we embrace
the tenets of The Book of Mormon, we whistle
while we work out our salvation, because of
the miracle of the Atonement. We learn how
our Heavenly Father has linked our own
efforts to those of His Son. Happiness,
as it turns out, is the object and
design of our existence, and it
will be the end thereof, if
we follow the path of
repentance that
leads to it.

Heavenly
angels who have ministered
on the earth in the latter-days for
the benefit of the children of God have
included Moroni, John the Baptist, as well
and Peter, James, and John, who, as messengers
of Jesus Christ, have restored true doctrine. Because
of the ministry of these and other servants, the prophets
have been able to declare with confidence that "no power on
earth or hell can overthrow or defeat that which God has
decreed. Every plan of the adversary will fail; for the
Lord knows the secret thoughts of men, and sees
the future with a vision clear and perfect,
even as though it were in the past."
(Joseph Fielding Smith, Jr.).

Over and over again, Book of Mormon prophets have taught that the hazmat protocol of repentance was written into God's Plan to detoxify us from the cares and habituating influences of the world, as well as from the homogenization process that occurs as we are worn down by the vicissitudes of life.

The Book of Mormon shows us precisely how to be repeatedly re-vitalized, as we are re-introduced to a Magical Kingdom in which our hopes and our dreams really will come true, if only we will muster the faith to wish upon a star that one cold winter night so long ago twinkled over a manger near Bethlehem.

The Book of
Mormon allows us to
be engaged and energized
as we journey through Idumea
at an unhurried and yet productive
pace. It captivates us by its simplicity,
but at the same time, we are immersed in
its intricacies, riveted by its rewards, and
wrapped up in its wonders. It patiently
anticipates our acknowledgement of
its ability to transform our lives
and guide us to the gates of
heaven, and it only waits
upon our initiative,
to do so.

What about those
of us who are not so sure
of ourselves? What happens
if we look in the mirror and
see only the face of a stranger
staring back at us? What if our
knees wobble at the prospect of the
leap of faith required as we tackle
The Book of Mormon, including
the Isaiah Chapters of Second
Nephi? We take comfort in
the way the Lord quieted
our fears, by simply
saying: "Be still,
and know that I
am God."

Because of The
Book of Mormon we're
more trusting of others,
and we speak without guile.
We are more transparent, and
we are less prejudicial. We have
fewer pretensions, and are more
genuine. We're far less prone to
rationalization, and quicker
to forgive. We are grounded
in many ways that bestow
upon us a heavenly peace
and a reassurance that
others cannot
know.

When we've nurtured
our relationship with the Holy
Ghost, He can be our mentor and
our teacher. If we are good students,
and have done our homework, He will
reward us with an illumination of the
truthfulness of The Book of Mormon
that will bathe our minds and our
spirits in a cascading current of
insight, intuition, inspiration
and revelation. He will give
us the answer key to the
exam that will follow
shortly on the heels
of the classes that
are a part of our
curriculum in
mortality.

Until it
has embraced The
Book of Mormon, our
society will remain on a
passage to self-destruction.
As we learn from D&C 1:16, it
seeks "not the Lord, to establish
his righteousness, but every man
walketh in his own way and after
the image of his own god, whose
image is in the likeness of the
world, and whose substance is
that of an idol which waxeth
old and shall perish in
Babylon ... which
shall fall."

There is a nearly
impenetrable veil that
has been drawn across our
minds. But we have The Book
of Mormon and the unimpeachable
witness of the Holy Ghost to assist us
in our efforts to probe that mysterious
curtain. In the interim, many of us are
swayed by Satan's siren song, drawn to
the duplicitous shoals of his spiritual
instability, thereon to founder, and
to be pulled under by the riptides
of religious relativism and the
undertow of agnosticism, or
faithless skepticism.

If the Nephite
warriors from Captain
Moroni's time had allowed
themselves to succumb to fear,
and had permitted faithlessness to
hobble the expression of their actions,
what would have been left in the end
would have been a monochromatic
and one-dimensional compromise
that left them with a hollow core
of emptiness in the pit of their
stomachs and terror in their
hearts. Faith, after all, is
fear that has said
its prayers.

It's when we read The
Book of Mormon that we will
feel the gentle caress of the hands
of the Master Potter, as He turns our
lives on the wheel of time. We'll give Him
permission, as the Artisan of our destiny, to
mold us and shape us. (See Jeremiah 18:6). We
are the clay, and He is our potter; and we are the
work of His hands. (See Isaiah 64:8). As our
thoughts turn to the Savior, we remain as
impressionable and pliable vessels to
the things of the Spirit, even tho
we are fired in the white-hot
oven of adversity.

"Be not troubled, for when all these things shall come to pass, ye may know that the promises which have been made unto you shall be fulfilled." (D&C 45:34-35). Prior to the Second Coming of Christ it will be as it was in the years before the birth of the Savior, when great signs were given in Zarahemla "to the intent that there should be no cause for unbelief," and also "to the intent that whosoever (would) believe might be saved." (Helaman 14:18-19). For now, the Savior has revealed Himself to all the world thru The Book of Mormon, but ultimately, He will do so "from heaven with power and great glory ... and dwell in righteousness with men on earth a thousand years." (D&C 29:11).

The Book of Mormon can safeguard us from spiritual identity theft. Of the truth that we have a Father in Heaven, there can be no question, for "the Spirit itself beareth witness with our spirit, that we are the children of God." (Romans 8:16). We know this intuitively, as do Primary age children as young as three years of age who sing the songs of Zion that proclaim the truth that every one of us is a child of God.

Every time we pause
in our busy lives to engage The
Book of Mormon, we are overcome with
enthusiasm, virtue garnishes our thoughts,
and our confidence is strong. The doctrine of the
priesthood distils upon our head as the dews from heaven,
the Holy Ghost is our constant companion, and the power to
reach our goals flows without compulsory means. We experience
spiritual delight, without the rush of sensory overstimulation that
is so prevalent in our technological world. As fire in the sky,
the air in our theater of life is charged with an electricity
that represents the inevitable merger of the universal
encouragement of the Light of Christ with the
pointed and providential guidance that
is provided by the Spirit.

Often, when we repent,
the Spirit will compel us to
jump from the frying pan right
into the fire. With practice, however,
when we make that leap of faith, we
will land on springboards to action
that will vault us upward toward
safety, so that we might balance
with confidence on pinnacles
of perfection that are found
in geographical references
throughout The Book
of Mormon.

We read The
Book of Mormon
to obtain a testimony
of the divinity of the work,
and to be liberated from fear,
uncertainty, the apprehension
of danger, religious turmoil,
and from the vagaries of
conspiring men and
women in the last
days.

The Book
of Mormon will
plot a safe passage
through the minefields
of mortality. It documents
potential perils and pitfalls,
charts the recommended route
that leads to refuge, maps out
the success strategies to which
we need to adhere if we desire
to live abundantly, and
measures our progress
on the pathway to
perfection.

Nothing can make up for the dogged discipline that is such a prominent feature of our Book of Mormon scholarship. Cheap thrills will not replace its lofty rewards, and novelty and spectacle cannot defeat, but only delay, implementation of its principles. The all-embracing influence of the Light of Christ inspires us to set our sights on the brightly burning beacon of the Holy Ghost, Who waits upon our initiative, to guide us across a vast ocean of light toward the discovery of a new world.

One of Satan's strategies is to lead the imprudent into improvident and profligate behavior with a flaxen cord around their necks that, at first, might actually feel quite comfortable. (See 2 Nephi 26:22). But once a habit pattern has been established, however, the unwary may be unpleasantly surprised to discover that they have sacrificed their agency to act independently, as they are bound under the yoke of sin by new routines that have taken hold and that are very difficult to change. Thus, does the Devil seek to bind us with his strong chains.

Opposition can become a powerful force, constantly refining us by pushing, pulling, and tearing away at us within the crucible of experience. On our own, we cannot eliminate the consequences of sin, which, unfortunately, is often the companion of opposition. For that to happen, The Book of Mormon re-introduces us to the Lamb of God Who was slain from the foundation of the world.

In The Book of Mormon, we are instructed how to establish a relationship with the Lord that is founded on covenants, to stand beside Him, and to weigh in on His side of the scale, even as the counterfeit coin of Satan's spurious currency clatters down in a cacophony of confusion on the other side of the scale.

The Book of Mormon repeatedly
illustrates how baptism comes with "the
remission of sins (which) bringeth meekness,
and lowliness of heart; and because of meekness
and lowliness of heart cometh the visitation of the
Holy Ghost, which Comforter filleth with hope
and perfect love, which love endureth by
diligence unto prayer, until the end
shall come, when all the saints
shall dwell with God."
(Moroni 8:26).

The powers of heaven and earth can
amplify each other and carry us along
on the waves of the Spirit, as we read The
Book of Mormon. Outward observances
and phylacteries are stripped from the
ritual of our worship, our trappings
and pretenses are shorn away,
and only our true feelings
remain, to be quickened
by the gentle touch
of the Holy
Ghost.

We have a burning desire to engage in a serious study of The Book of Mormon because of our testimonies that its principles, doctrines, ordinances, and covenants were among the "great and eternal purposes (that) were prepared from the foundation of the world." (Alma 42:26). Our baptism itself testifies that we were willing then, and are eager now, to ratify and participate in God's great Plan of Happiness.

Alma taught: "For behold, it is as easy to give heed to the word of Christ, which will point to you a straight course to eternal bliss, as it was for our fathers to give heed to this compass, which would point unto them a straight course to the promised land." (Alma 37: 44). As it was for Alma and his people, so it is for us. The Book of Mormon has become our 'rudder', and the Savior is our Navigator. If we follow it, and Him, and allow them to guide us to the waters of baptism, we'll find that there is no wind that can blow except it fills our sails.

The basis of our foundation in the Kingdom of God is grounded on the footings of saving faith, as was the wall that was built by an Irishman around his farm. When asked why he had built it five feet high and eight feet thick, he explained that if the wind ever blew so hard that it would topple over, his wall of protection would still be five feet thick. The Book of Mormon does the same thing. It shelters us with the shield of faith, enabling us to withstand any wind that blows, no matter how ferocious it might seem to be.

We retain an abiding faith in the Book of Mormon's glorious promise that, because of our baptismal covenant, one day in the not-too-distant future, the atmosphere that we breathe will be pungent with a heavenly ether that is punctuated by the melodious strains of a lively conversation in our native tongue. Each detail is exactly as we had imagined it, including the heat radiating from a reassuring celestial fire that has been kindled beforehand by Father, in preparation for our homecoming.

We are baptized
so that the Spirit of the
Lord Omnipotent might work
"a mighty change in us, or in
our hearts, that we have no more
disposition to do evil, but to
do good continually."
(Mosiah 5:2).

As they
were baptized,
angels attended the
faithful Nephites. "For
I will go before your face,"
promised the Savior. "I will
be on your right hand, and on
your left, and my Spirit shall be
in your hearts, and mine angels
round about you, to bear you up."
(D&C 84:88). With such a promise,
they determined never to turn their
backs on such an outpouring of
spiritual fortification, return
to their wicked ways, and
try to make it on their
own.

Those timid souls who remain cautiously hesitant and tentatively faithful don't consciously intend to ignore the spiritual promptings that urge them to embrace the teachings of The Book of Mormon. Their faith to believe just fades away, as does the slow leak in a bike tire, rather than as a blowout.

The awesome spiritual gift of the interpretation of tongues includes our capacity to comprehend the words of the scriptures, including those of The Book of Mormon, as well as the inspired counsel that flows from the lips of those who sit in the presiding quorums of the church. Clearly and unambiguously, the Plan has been designed to perfectly meet our needs.

Our eternal welfare depends upon how we handle opposition, and on what we allow it to do to us. It may impede our progress; but on the other hand, we may use it as a stepping-stone to higher achievement. The Book of Mormon helps us to have the perspective to see adversity as a diamond dust that can polish us to a high luster, rather than as an abrasive that wears us down and grinds us up.

The doctrine found on nearly every page in The Book of Mormon constitutes "the words of eternal life" (John 6:63) and when followed, it has the power to emancipate us from the self-limiting conditions that had heretofore blinded us to a larger view of life. It will free us to pay close attention to celestial guideposts and principles. It invites us to experience more intense and reflective self-awareness, deeper and more abiding humility, reinvigorated confidence, and incomprehensibly more profound and enduring faith in our Lord and Savior Jesus Christ. Its doctrine has the power to make our lives sublime as they turn on the hands of time.

The Book of Mormon endows us with power to follow the Savior "with full purpose of heart, acting no hypocrisy and no deception before God." (2 Nephi 31:13). When we do so, the night of our darkness will be followed by a renaissance, a spiritual rebirth paving the way for enlightenment. Our world will blossom with new ideas and with unbridled optimism, and we will realize that it is we of whom Isaiah spoke. Although we once walked in darkness, we have now seen a great light. We dwelt in the valley of the shadow of death, but now, the Holy Ghost traces a flaming trajectory as it streaks across our horizons. (See Isaiah 9:2).

In The Book of Mormon, the anchors of our faith rest upon a foundation of rock, rather than of sand. Our testimonies are composed of three essential elements. First is our conscious recognition of gospel principles. Secondly, is our understanding of word of the Lord concerning the principles. Finally, is our direct experience with the principles, which we call the fruits of faith.

If we no
longer believe in
The Book of Mormon,
we must concede that our
skepticism is attributable to
a lack of faith that initiated the
flat spin from which we could not
recover. Blame for the demolition of
our discipleship, not to mention the
chain-reaction of unfortunate and
inevitable consequences that will
surely follow, must rest at our
own doorstep. When we try to
shift that blame to others,
we are only deluding
ourselves.

The Great
Plan of the Eternal
God dictates that there will
come for each one of us a great
and dreadful day when we will be
asked to stand and give our sworn
deposition before God, angels, and
witnesses. (See Alma 5:22). Upon
the issue of faith, depending upon
our answer, we will be counted
among the sheep or the goats,
and find ourselves on His
right hand, or on His
left hand.

It is within
the pages of The
Book of Mormon that we
will encounter a description of
the only truly effective shield of
protection against a corrosive spatter
of perspiration that is cast about by the
Devil, who pervasively and persistently
works overtime in a concentrated effort
to damage our doctrinal defenses, dull
our spiritual sensitivities, diminish
our charitable capacity, deplete
our bountiful reservoirs of
sympathy, and destroy
our devotions. (See
3 Nephi 4:30).

In The Book of Mormon, every
time that the Nephites fortified themselves
with righteousness, they were insulated from
the influences of the world that would have otherwise
left them vulnerable to the enticements of him who is the
adversary of all that is good. The terrible effect of sin on those
who had previously been taught the principles of the gospel was
that the guidance of the Spirit was withdrawn, and they were left
alone to grope in darkness. Guilt caused them to shrink from
church activity, and in the absence of the Spirit, sinners
had no claim on blessings, prosperity, or preservation.
Tragically, those individuals, feeling uncomfortable
in proximity to spiritual experiences, withdrew to
lifestyles devoid of such associations. Thus
began a downward spiral that gained
momentum as sinful practices,
more easily committed,
became habitual.

Book of
Mormon principles
make it far easier to have
lips that have learned how to
articulate nothing but positive
expressions of speech and that
never speak guile, and shoulders
that have developed the strength
to bear the burdens of those who
have been battered and bruised
by the vicissitudes of life and
who are staggering under
the weight of sorrow or
unresolved sin.

Heavenly Father's Great and Eternal
Plan of Deliverance from Death (see 2 Nephi
11:5) has provisions that have been etched into its
blueprints, stipulating that guidance from heaven will
come to us in the form of subtle impressions and spiritual
promptings that are more common that one might suspect.
Powerful intuitive communicators influence us to push
forward in the direction of our dreams, toward the faith
to believe, that blesses us with a greater appreciation
of the concern of our Savior for each of us, which
brings us back to an equally significant
name for His divine design, which is
The Great Plan of Happiness.
(See Alma 42:8).

We need
to venture forth
out from the shadows,
relying upon the guidance
that we receive from the Light
of Christ and from the ministering
of angels, if we want to experience the
special familiarity that the faithful enjoy
with the Lord of all the earth, and with "the
Great Plan of The Eternal God" of which,
and of Whom. the Spirit regularly
testifies. (Alma 39:4).

When
it's our time
to come face to
face with eternity,
(see Moroni 10:34), the
principles of the Plan will
catalyze our transformation
from mortal clay into "a better
and an enduring substance."
(Hebrews 10:34). Still, for as
long as we remain trapped in
bodies, we'll find that we are
capable of only indirectly
appreciating the eternal
scope of God's divine
design for each of
His children.

As we study,
and we learn precept
by precept, here a little
and there a little, the details
relating to the Great Plan that
God has devised for us, we realize
that we can become the architects of
our own destiny. But it also dawns on
us just how much we have borrowed from
our Lord Jesus Christ, as well as from the
towering examples of the prophets of The
Book of Mormon who have always been
our mystical mentors, as well as our
sensible chaperones, our spiritual
guides, our surrogate saviors,
our compassionate critics,
and our spiritual
guides.

If, as
we study The
Book of Mormon,
we have unknowingly
taken poetic license with
the foundation principles of
the book, or if we have needlessly
added ecclesiastical embroidery to
gospel truths, we risk diminishing
the intensity of our faith to believe,
and we must speedily repent, and
modify our approach to worship
and scholarship.

Armed
with our faith in
The Book of Mormon,
our innermost longings
to apprehend visions of the
eternal worlds are epitomized
by our triumphant realization of
dreams fulfilled. In the expression
of our testimonies, our emotions will
be painted by the words that depict our
progression toward distant mileposts
that mark the way we must all go as
we trudge along through the vast
wastelands of Idumea, past the
great and spacious buildings
of Babylon, on our way
to keep our date with
destiny.

The Book of Mormon
has the power to surprise us in
myriad and delightful ways. It
cultivates a culture of reflection,
keeps the Savior in our thoughts,
nurtures an eternal perspective,
and initiates positive change,
as obedience to its principles
helps us to harmonize our
our actions with the
order of heaven.

The Book of
Mormon gives us
tools to watch ourselves
judiciously, that we might
be the meticulous guardians
of our thoughts, the scrupulous
custodians of our words, and the
prudent caretakers of our actions.
We fastidiously observe the laws of
God, that we might benefit from the
stability of a pathway that basks
in the steady illumination that
has been generously supplied
by the dynamo of faith.

It is
all too easy to
talk about our faith
in The Book of Mormon
timidly or superficially by
retreating into tasteless and
colorless verbiage as the easy
way out. We take care that we
are not steering a course that
would take us away from the
Savior by any inconsiderate,
thoughtless, or dismissive
expressions that might
betray a weakness
in the armor of
our faith.

If we've never allowed the stories from The Book of Mormon to give us the strength to endure the hard lessons that life throws our way with frustrating frequency, we'll look elsewhere for gods of wood and stone to heal our temporal trauma. But at our core, we'll know that these quick fixes could never permanently redeem us from our misery.

If we are too busy to frequently study The Book of Mormon, it is likely because we have become absorbed in puerile activities that concentrate on obtaining, accumulating, consolidating, and securing our material interests. The problem with that juvenile approach to life is that the eternal welfare of our souls continues to hang in the balance, no matter where our priorities may lie.

The Book
of Mormon
orders our chaotic
world, bequeathing
our lives with clarity
rather than confusion.
It simply teaches us how
to achieve fluency in the
intuitive language of
the Spirit.

Those who
unwisely drink of the
wine of the wrath of God
have been enslaved by selfish
indulgences and "regard not the
work of the Lord, neither consider the
operation of his hands." (2 Nephi 15:12).
Without the knowledge of His ways, they
are captive. They are "famished, and their
multitude dried up with thirst. Therefore,
hell hath enlarged herself, and opened
her mouth without measure; and their
glory, and their multitude, and their
pomp, and he that rejoiceth, shall
descend into it (even as) God
that is holy (is) sanctified
in (His) righteousness."
(2 Nephi 15:13-16).

The Book of Mormon has the power to bless our lives with self-shaping, self-supporting, self-sustaining and self-renewing characteristics. At its center, its doctrine becomes a perfectly liberating law that allows us to reach our potential in an atmosphere of mutually supportive inter-dependency with the Savior. His work and glory become our quest for the holy grail of immortality and eternal life in the Celestial Kingdom.

Those who are of weak character think that they might somehow find ways to circumvent the performance requirements of The Book of Mormon, but this is because they have never enjoyed the experiences of those who claim the strait and narrow way as their home turf. They mistake wicked behavior for happiness, because they confuse nature with nobility.

Young
people talk
about being "Best
Friends Forever," but
Heavenly Father would
rather have us "Be Forever
Faithful" through the bonds
of obedience to the principles,
doctrines, ordinances, and
covenants of The Book
of Mormon.

Within the embrace of group
study of the magnificent themes
running thru The Book of Mormon,
conformity can provide each member
with significant sustainable support.
Without the consistency that is one of
the greatest blessings of fellowship, our
lives might spiral downward in a flat
spin. Such is the condition of those
who are confronted by the sense of
futility that accompanies their
failure to concentrate on the
innate upward reach of
the gospel.

Although we're incapable of saving our daylight time, we may try to maximize it by strangling ourselves with the things that we can buy, whose opacity obstructs our ability to see what is really there. In fact, we aren't on daylight savings time at all, but rather on Book of Mormon time. We observe the Lord' agenda, for we are on His errand no matter how long it might take, or how preoccupied by the distractions and trivial concerns of the world we may have become.

The Book of Mormon teaches that our road to repentance will follow a natural progression, but the real power that stems from the Atonement and saves us from our sins hinges upon a deeper and more abiding faith. It's "the substance of things hoped for, the evidence of things not seen." (Hebrews 11:1).

The Holy Ghost
sees thru the clarifying
and purifying lens of eternity,
and from a unique vantage point
He will bless our lives as He nurtures
our testimony of The Book of Mormon.
The veil that has been drawn before our
eyes only for a moment prevents us
from experiencing eternity from
the unobstructed viewpoint of
the thousand years of
Nephite history.

The
Book of Mormon
teaches that were it
not for the Atonement of
Christ, we would be devoid of
the blessings we receive because
of our obedience to covenants, and
we would remain miserable, living
in a state of separation not only
from the presence of our Father
in Heaven, but also from His
only begotten Son, as well
as from the Holy
Ghost.

The Book of Mormon
stimulates us to examine
what it means to be anxiously
engaged. It inspires us to plumb
the depths of our commitment to the
Savior. It sensitizes us to the nobility
of His work, expands upon our visions of
immortality, personalizes His Atonement,
and encourages us to remain consciously
aware of God's promise of immortality
and eternal life, and of our close
proximity to heaven.

It is
in The Book
of Mormon where
we learn that Jesus
Christ is the Father of
our spiritual regeneration
and like the parent that we
all aspire to be, He is there to
heal our infirmities and bind
up our wounds, every time we
stumble and whenever we fall,
because of the weight we have
been attempting to carry by
ourselves. Even though we
may forget all about Him,
He will never, no never,
forget about us.

The more righteous individuals among the Nephites bound themselves to the heavens by their obedience, initializing a pulsing stream of inspiration whose flow knew neither temporal boundaries nor spatial limitations. When they were bad, they were very bad, but when they were good, they were at one with the mind and will of God.

Since there must needs be opposition, even as there is faith, so must there also be its worldly counterpart. In our day, the awful grip of fear paralyzes many of God's children. Today, more than ever, we need a hope in Christ. We need the assurance of peace, that our lives are moving in the direction of our dreams. In The Book of Mormon, we can learn how to lasso the stars.

The
Book of
Mormon shows
how to see with the
eye of faith, as thru
a spiritual prism. It's
principles will touch us,
so that we may learn to see
beyond the limited horizon
of our sight, all the way into
the eternities. By the power of
the Holy Ghost, our eyes will
will be opened, that we may
begin to understand the
reach of the Savior's
influence on our
lives.

It is our faith that binds
together the doctrinal building
blocks that are found within The
Book of Mormon's pages. Without
it, the fabric of our lives unravels in
a process leading to disintegration.
When the anchor of the knowledge
of the Plan of God is missing, our
experiences can be like a train
wreck in slow motion that is
frustratingly repeated
over and over.

We
are blessed
to internalize
the doctrine between
the covers of The Book
of Mormon, but only after
our faith has been religiously
recalibrated thru repentance. It
allows us to become reinvigorated
by the refreshing breeze of celestial
air. Its teachings paint a portrait of
free-will where we may take risks. If,
in our efforts, we fail to measure up
to our obligations, Jesus Christ will
always step in to intervene in our
behalf by using the bargaining
chip of His Atonement in order
to placate the unrelenting
demands of Justice.

When the prophets of The Book of
Mormon have re-introduced us to those noble
principles that guided us during our spiritual
kindergarten years in the pre-earth existence,
we will be blessed with a focus of faith that
will accompany us throughout the process
of our return to that more natural
state of harmony with the
heavens.

Mormon taught us that obstacles are frightful demons that threaten us when we take our minds off the Atonement. They loom large with a gratuitous significance. It is faith that endows us with the vision to see beyond these potential stumbling blocks. If we turn them into stepping stones to pave the way to our higher achievement, it will be because we've been empowered by the capacity of our faith in Jesus Christ, that is an unrestrained and creative engine that drives positive change. His truth will make us free. (See John 8:32).

Sooner or later, each of us must undertake a journey that will lead to The Book of Mormon. As we move along the Yellow Brick Road thru the forest of faith toward the Emerald City of Oz, we use the brains we've been given to instill our hearts with courage, all the while remembering that the woods would be very quiet if no birds sang but those that sang best.

Without
knowledge,
there can be no
faith; without faith,
there can be no light,
and without light there
will be no recognition of
religious truth; and without
spiritual enlightenment, when
just one of these three elements
of faith, light, and truth is lost,
then all must be forsaken. Our
fortunes rest upon the basis of
how completely we internalize
this fundamental teaching
of the prophets from The
Book of Mormon.

The Book
of Mormon is as
our celestial compass,
calibrated by God's finger.
It is oriented toward the truth,
and it is always available to guide
the faithful to a safe haven. It is also
there for those who have lost their way,
to bring them into the fold of the Good
Shepherd, and to show others how they
might return to the sanctuary and
security of the community of
Christ from which they
may have strayed.

Those who
decline to nurture and
then maintain a deep and
abiding faith in the doctrinal
truth of The Book of Mormon lack
spiritual horsepower. Their dearth of
traction is awkwardly apparent while
the inability to generate spontaneity
is palpable, and their lack of energy
to engage enthusiasm is noticeable.
Their incapacity to spark vitality
is apparent, and their failure to
unabashedly acknowledge the
dynamic relationship that
can exist between God
and themselves is
undisputed.

Sooner or
later, each of us,
as a child of God, must
discover for ourselves that a
line has been drawn in the sand.
If we then act upon the promptings
of the Holy Ghost to seize the power of
The Book of Mormon, we will generate
the positive energy that will move us
inexorably forward in the direction
of our dreams. Those with the faith
to rely upon the merits of Christ,
of Whom the book so boldly
testifies, will cross that
line and be saved in
the Kingdom
of God.

We receive no witness until after the trial of our faith. Having said that, those with little or no faith will characteristically throw up defensive dross that is designed to deflect, disrespect, disregard, discourage, or even disparage the power of The Book of Mormon. They may be enthusiastic, but they are still ignorant.

How we go about generating the faith to believe in The Book of Mormon will either deify or destroy us. Our response to the Savior's entreaties to come unto Him will delineate our dreams, and define our destiny. It will determine how, where and with whom we will spend all eternity. We can almost hear the voice of the Lord as He exclaims: 'Carpe diem!'

There will
come for each one of
us a great and dreadful
day, when we will be asked
to stand and give our sworn
testimony before God, angels, and
witnesses. On the issue of faith in The
Book of Mormon, Another Testament of
Christ, depending upon our statement, we
will be counted among the sheep or the goats,
and find ourselves on His right hand, or on
His left hand. We should begin thinking
about how we will respond to the gentle
inquiry: "What think ye of Christ?"
and "What think ye of The
Book of Mormon?"

The Book of Mormon helps us to be slow to be led
to do iniquity. There must needs be opposition in all
things, but even the righteous can be seduced by corrosive
cocktails of convenience, adroitly offered by a bartender named
Beelzebub. The Devil's designer drinks are poisonous potions whose
naturally bitter taste is attenuated by all of his counterfeits
concoctions and potions, such as pleasure, decadence,
indulgence, hedonism, intemperance,
and self-gratification.

The Book of
Mormon, and in
particular the book of
Third Nephi, reminds us
of the suffering of our Savior
when He took upon Himself the
heavy burden of our sins, and so
it stimulates our own soul-sweat.
It works upon our sense of duty,
on our conscience, and on our
scruples, and it persistently
persuades us to act on our
faith, so that not our
will, but that of
God, might be
done.

The wicked Lamanite
brethren of the Nephites, who
would not repent, retained a taste
for fast food that had been heated up
in a sensory microwave. It was only
outwardly appealing and was full of
empty calories. When the Lamanites
measured the missionaries and their
message of salvation, they tended
to see darkly, through a filter of
worldly pollution that had been
desperately, but superficially,
whitewashed to cover up the
underlying canker in
their character.

One of the
blessings that continues
to flow from our unequivocal
acceptance of The Book of Mormon,
is our concurrent receipt of a constant
stream of inspiration that cascades down
from the heavens. This ensures that we will
walk along illuminated pathways guided
by the only institution that has the right
to legitimately claim that it receives
revelation, and that's been given
God's approbation, even The
Church of Jesus Christ
of Latter-day
Saints.

Because Mormon
knew that Babylon's
image consultants would
confuse the weightier matters
of the law in the tumultuous Last
Days, he cautioned us to "take heed,
that (we) not judge that which is evil to
be of God, or that which is good and of God
to be of the devil." (Moroni 7:14). In the vast
arena of the world, there are no shades of gray
for those who have not only received the Light
of Christ, but also the greater light of the Holy
Ghost. For to them it is given "to judge, that
(they) may know good from evil; and the
way to judge is as plain, that ye may
know with a perfect knowledge, as
the daylight is from the dark
night." (Moroni 7:15).

The
Book of Mormon
furnishes us with more
than enough tools to satisfy
all of the entrance requirements
for admittance into the kingdom.
We couldn't be blessed with a greater
gift to help us to do so than the Holy
Ghost, Who can be our willing and
capable Teacher and Mentor.

Every
one of us has
been exposed to a
constant stream of
insight and intuition,
as well as of inspiration
and revelation, that flow in
a cascade of creativity from
their Source. Divine guidance
blesses all of us to walk along
illuminated pathways and to
execute our faculties of mind
and spirit, to better utilize
The Book of Mormon to
meet the challenges
of the day.

There are unseen legions of an angelic host who have come down from the throne of God to visit the earth. They have included Moroni and John the Baptist, as well as Peter, James and John. As messengers of Jesus Christ, they have restored true doctrine. Because of the ministry of these and other servants, a prophet has been able to confidently declare that "no power on earth or hell can overthrow or defeat that which God has decreed. Every plan of the adversary will fail, for the Lord knows the secret thoughts of men, and sees the future with a vision clear and perfect, even as though it were in the past." (Joseph Fielding Smith, Jr.).

The Book of Mormon safeguards the stability of the divine center of faith. The energy we expend to cultivate its sense of permanency, prevents our world from collapsing into disarray or imploding under the dreadful weight of unresolved sin.

Book
of Mormon
credos envelop
us in an intuitive
appreciation of where
we have come from, the
tangible element of why
we are here, as well as the
revelatory reassurance
of where we are
going.

It won't be easy for
those who've turned their
backs on their testimony of
the Plan of Salvation and of
The Book of Mormon to obtain
forgiveness. Those who will no
longer allow Christ into their
lives will die in their sins.
Without repentance, they
cannot be saved in the
Kingdom of God.

The Book of Mormon prepares us for our journey along a pathway that leads to the Kingdom of God. We await the further light and knowledge that He has promised to send to us through His prophets.

As if they were our spiritual swaddling clothes, the threads of faith that have been woven into our coats of many colors reverberate with intrinsic light from The Book of Mormon. It radiates in a pulsing stream that follows a path all the way to a witness of the Spirit.

As we reflect
upon the ramifications
of both our lineage and of
our birthright, that we learn
about in The Book of Mormon,
we might want to consider our
own covenant consciousness.
We might forget that we, too,
are members of the House of
Israel, either literally or by
adoption, and that we too
may claim the covenant
blessings promised by
God so long ago, not
only to Abraham,
but also, to all
of his seed.

We read in the
scriptures that those
who have repented and
become the Lord's disciples
are figuratively characterized
as "white, fair, and beautiful."
(1 Nephi 13:5). Moroni used the
terms "spotless, pure, fair, and
white." (Mormon 9:6). These
are those who symbolically
have been cleansed by the
blood of the Lamb, in a
rite of purification in
a tale that is as old
as time itself.

One of the
terrible consequences
of the fascination of Babylon
with telestial titillation, and with
its fixation on the vain and trifling
images of the world, is its insensitivity
to spiritual impressions and whisperings
that it might have received had it been even
remotely interested in learning more about
the eternity-altering ramifications having
to do with internalizing the doctrine and
principles that are clearly illustrated
by the prophets of God who bore their
testimonies in nearly every
chapter of The Book
of Mormon.

Those
of us to whom has
been given the supernal
gift of The Book of Mormon
sometimes leave it untouched
and undisturbed in its original
packaging. We seem to forget that
the Savior will always be there to
help us make important choices
and keep our promises, as we
engage the principles of
God's great Plan of
Salvation.

Throughout The Book of Mormon, we are
taught that the Atonement has prepared a petition
that is to be submitted to the court of Justice, seeking a
summary dismissal of all of the charges that have been
lodged against us. Our trial proceedings have already
been docketed to follow the conclusion of our mortal
experience. To avoid a reversal of our fortunes, we
must pay our Advocate the retainer of a broken
heart and a contrite spirit, for He is even
now preparing to plead our case at
the commencement of that
heavenly tribunal.

Each one of the willing
participants in life's Three Act
Play is now and forever independent
in that stage of development to which their
decisions have led them. Poised at the edge of
forever, they need little incentive other than the
encouragement of Moroni (see Moroni 10:32)
to cast themselves off in the direction of the
unknown possibilities of existence, where
they will seek out new life and new
civilizations, and boldly go to a
place where no one but the
faithful have gone
before.

It is God's work and glory for all His children, sooner or later, to make their way to Christ, and a good way to do that is to start right now and follow the guidance provided in The Book of Mormon. If they do that, it will be as it was during the reign of King Josiah, who "went up into the house of the Lord, and all the men of Judah and all the inhabitants of Jerusalem with him, and the priests, and the prophets, and all the people, both small and great. And (they) made a covenant before the Lord, to walk after the Lord, and to keep his commandments and his testimonies and his statutes with all their heart and all their soul, (and) to perform the words of the covenant. And all the people stood to the covenant."
(2 Kings 23:2-3).

As we internalize the scriptures, and we consider the elements of all of the references to God's Creation, that are found in The Book of Mormon, for example, in 1 Nephi 17:36, 2 Nephi 2:14 & 29:7, Jacob 2:21 & 4:9, Mosiah 2:21, 3:8 4:9 & 7:27, & Alma 18:28-32, it seems that our faith should remain fixed on the revelations the Lord has given us that relate to our world, and not on mysteries that have not been revealed to us, may never be revealed, or that just may not be pertinent to our current circumstances.

In every epoch
of the world, the tender
shoots of budding testimony
have sprung up and have been
carefully nurtured in accord with
Alma's inspired formula (see Alma
Chapter 30) without the ecclesiastical
embroidery that too often needlessly
complicates the simple sewing, and
the sowing, of the messages
of the gospel.

The poetry of The Book
of Mormon may be used as
a springboard to reach elevated
plateaus of discovery, as we are
taught by the Spirit to think
as Israelites do, and jump
off in the direction of
our dreams.

Valiant souls who
are firm in their faith
and believe that The Book
of Mormon is yet Another
Testament of Jesus Christ,
will find that heaven will
come knocking at their
door. When it does,
they will get up
and open
it.

While they drew, a kindergarten teacher
walked up and down the rows of students in her
class, observing her pupils' work. She paused at the
desk of a little girl and asked what she was drawing.
She replied: "I'm drawing a picture of God." The teacher
paused, and then tentatively said: "But no one knows
what He looks like." Without missing a beat, or even
looking up from her paper, the girl said: "They
will in a minute." Though she was tender in
years, this child had faith (and her
parents had probably read
The Book of Mormon
to her).

If we want to capture the blessings that are revealed within the sacramental prayers that are spelled out with exactness in Moroni Chapters 4 & 5, to always have the Spirit to be with us, we need to experience how the Holy Ghost manifests personal revelation. "For God speaketh once, yea twice, yet man perceiveth it not. In a dream, in a vision of the night, when deep sleep falleth upon men, in slumberings upon the bed; then he openeth the ears of men, and sealeth their instruction." (Job 33:4-16).

If it is our desire to sustain our focus of faith while we investigate the claims made by The Book of Mormon, we won't get in the thick of thin things. We'll cultivate an equilibrium centered away from the madding crowd and at a safe distance that's far from the ego-filled minds of mediocre men. We'll do our best to insulate ourselves from the confusion and tumult of the world, in the hope that we might enjoy a firmness that is unshakable.

If we read
The Book of Mormon
to gain a testimony of
the truth, we'll face the sun,
that we might feel the warmth
of its rays upon our cheeks, listen
with greater sensitivity, hear the word
of the Lord without ambiguity, and see
with a lucidity that encourages us to turn
a deaf ear to those who are at different mile
posts on their own journeys, who curse the
darkness at noonday, lament that the
heavens are silent, and teach that
prophecy has ceased to exist.

Those with the
faith to have become
the beneficiaries of God's
divine intervention, and who
have put Moroni's challenge to
the test, have been touched by
angels, and have in many
other ways been blessed
to walk in the light
of the Lord.

All of those who have forsaken
the world to faithfully embrace The Book
of Mormon, adopt the gospel of Jesus Christ, and
internalize the lifestyle of Latter-day Saints, have
experienced spiritual heart transplants. Therefore,
anti-rejection protocols must be rigorously
observed after they have been given
their new hearts, and have
been born again.

When he spoke to members of the church
who dwelt in Corinth, the apostle Paul painted a
vivid portrait of our own second mile commitment
of faith after we have gained a testimony of The Book
of Mormon and the great latter-day work. He asserted
that we "are manifestly declared to be the epistle of
Christ ministered by us, written not with ink,
but with the Spirit of the living God; (and
not just) in tables of stone, but (also)
in fleshy tables of the heart."
(2 Corinthians 3:3).

As we study The
Book of Mormon and our
minds and our hearts begin to
grasp the nature of God, we learn
more about how we fit in to His divine
design. We discover how faith drives the
law into our inward parts. We intuitively
sense this, and when the process has been
accomplished, in one of His miracles, the
articles of our faith will have become the
particles of our faith, and we will have
become new creatures in Christ, in a
process of generation, and not
just of maturation.

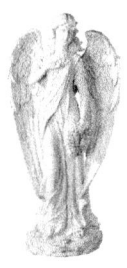

The
tendency
toward turmoil
is a tell-tale sign that
the Deceiver is lurking in
the shadows, lying in wait to
disrupt the poise of those who are
pressing forward in the direction of
the dreams that lie at the core of their
divine center of faith, as they lift the
latch and force the way, ponder and
pray, and study the monumental
themes that are found in The
Book of Mormon.

The prophet-historians of The Book of Mormon provide us with the practical skills that teach us how to express ourselves through positive and independent action, while the courage of faith introduces us to the exhilarating feeling of freedom from incarceration to sin that we can only experience when we have been obedient to a Higher Power and we have repented of our sins through the Atonement of Christ.

There are those who are in our midst who are nothing more than modern scribes and Pharisees. They have little or no faith, and omit the weightier matters of the law, including the metal plates from which The Book of Mormon was translated by the gift and power of God. They strain at a gnat, and swallow a camel, appearing to be pious, but inside they are "full of extortion and excess." (Matthew 23:25). At the other end of the spectrum, it's the righteous desire of the pure in heart to exercise the wisdom of faith to bring themselves closer to the Savior, leaving very little room for hypocrisy to creep into their lives. Somehow, they have managed to forge a spiritual bond with the Infinite.

The Savior's ministry among the Nephites after His resurrection from the dead may be one the greatest miracles of all, but those who deny the Lord's divinity cannot be saved on His merits alone, because they have not generated faith with enough power to carry their progression onward. Only a profound attitude adjustment that takes into consideration every element of the Plan of Salvation will jump-start their discipleship with enough forward momentum to carry them along the pathway that leads right to the Kingdom of God.

The Book of Mormon will gently soothe our spirits with the inexplicable images of religious recognition, touching our heartstrings and creating harmonic chords whose music remind us of our noble birthright.

"Behold, the field was ripe," cried Ammon to his brethren Aaron, Omner, and Himni, "and blessed are ye, for ye did thrust in the sickle, and did reap with your might, yea, all the day long did ye labor (for fourteen long years!) and behold the number of your sheaves!" (Alma 26:5). His party had come up out of the Land of Zarahemla into the highlands of Nephi to bring a message of love to the Lamanites. In the absence of that message, their kinsmen "would still have been racked with hatred (against the Nephites), and they would also have (remained) strangers to God." (Alma 26:9).

In a way that is contrary to The Book of Mormon ability to nurture the development of personality traits that are harmonious, or in balance, with the symmetry of heaven, sinful behavior is harmful because it interferes with our capacity to nurture the equilibrium that is a defining characteristic of those who strive to inherit eternal life. In our deeds, there must be neither variableness, nor can God tolerate even the hint of a "shadow of turning." (James 1:17).

Zenos
foresaw
that Israel,
characterized
by the natural
branches that had
grown wild, would be
grafted in to the natural
tree in a spiritual rebirth.
The roots and the branches
would be equal in strength,
as they were nourished by the
word of the Lord, receiving line
line upon line and precept upon
precept. Covenant Israel, or the
Gentiles, would grow up beside
Blood Israel with a testimony
of the Lord. In the millennial
day, it will no longer be as
before, when the branches
had grown at a faster
rate than the roots
could bear.

God never promised the Nephites
skies always blue or flower strewn pathways
all their lives through. Nor has He promised sun
without rain, joy without sorrow, or peace without
pain. But He did promise them strength for the
day, rest from their labors, and light for the
way, grace for their trials, help from above,
unfailing sympathy, and undying
love. (Anonymous).

We are
encouraged
in The Book of
Mormon to be perfect
in our repentance, that
God might give us the spirit
of wisdom and of revelation to
enlighten our understanding, so
that we might embrace a hope of the
high calling of Jesus Christ. Chariots
of fire will then carry us into heaven,
where we will commune with angelic
beings, the general assembly, and
the church of the Firstborn.
(See 3 Nephi 28:13).

Because of the
Atonement of Christ,
we might remember our
transgressions of the law
of God only in the positive
sense that our testimony is
increased. With the principle
of opposition in all things, our
Father in Heaven uses both sin
and repentance to strengthen
us to be more stalwart soldiers
in the army of Christ. (Nephi
2:11, see Alma Chapter 42).
Thus, even our disobedience
will ultimately accrue to
our benefit as well as to
God's advantage.

When
we have prayed
about the grand themes
that are found within in The
Book of Mormon, our faith will
convict us of our sins. Then, as we
approach the font, we'll bow our heads
in reverence. The words of the baptismal
prayer will orient our thoughts on the stars
and lift them to eternity, no matter where we
may have been bobbing about on the vast ocean
of life. Initially, getting a fix on the symbolism
that will come alive with intentional imagery and
magical metaphor might seem daunting to us. But
soon, the timeless messages that are conveyed by the
Spirit and have come down from the wide expanse
of eternity, will descend as the dews of heaven.
They will transcend time, will peacefully
rest upon our minds, and will loom
larger than life itself.

Once we have read The
Book of Mormon, have prayed
about it, and have received our own
witness of its divine authenticity, we
will have little inclination to look back
as we flee the lifestyle of Sodom and the
temptations of Gomorrah. We will leave
the ranks of those who have nestled
themselves into vacation retreats
in Babylon, even though their
home address may still be
somewhere in Zion.

Those who surrender their dreams and deny the miraculous origin of The Book of Mormon sell their birthright to the lowest bidder for a mess of pottage. Once they have made the exchange, they may far too easily be dragged down to a hell on earth, where, with terror, they realize that it is with the spurious currency of the Devil, that great deceiver, that they've purchased and then decorated the prison cell into which they have unceremoniously been cast.

Our acceptance of The Book of Mormon as canon scripture commits us to the arduous process of choosing the harder right, that is accompanied by a spiritual rebirth. Its alternative would leave us to follow a wobbly course that leads to the easier wrong. But that is a devilish detour that is characterized by the desire to subvert the Plan of God by forcing the capitulation by Mercy to the miscarriage of Justice, wherein we would somehow be saved in our sins.

If we allow
it to work its magic,
The Book of Mormon will
charge the air in the theater
of life as fire in the sky, with
an electricity that represents the
inevitable merger of the universal
encouragement of the Light of
Christ, with the pointed and
providential guidance of
the Holy Ghost, that is
God's gift of faith
to believe.

Our
attempts to
comprehend the
doctrine of The Book
of Mormon help us to
understand ourselves. It
is when we have discovered
the answers to where we came
from and why we are here that
we'll be prepared to embark upon
the incredible journey into our
future, to see with the eye of
faith just where it is that
we are going.

With faith
to embrace the
harder right, while
distaining the easier
wrong, we will avoid the
world's amusement parks,
and will gratefully utilize
the aid stations described in
The Book of Mormon that have
been providentially provided
for the use of Zion. We will
adapt its teachings to be
as celestial barometers
that are calibrated to a
scale that measures
the capacity of
our hearts.

The Book
of Mormon is like
a fire in our bones, and it
causes our blood to run hot. It
is reminiscent of the microwave
background radiation which is an
ever-present reminder of the creation
of our universe billions of years ago,
as well as of the fiery cauldrons of
experience that were catalyzed in
a garden setting eastward in
Eden, that was not so
very long ago.

In
The Book
of Mormon,
(3 Nephi 9:15), we
learn that it was Jesus
Christ, under the direction
of our Father in Heaven Who
created the earth upon which we
stand as a learning laboratory, and
as a telestial testing center. It would
be a citadel of higher education, and a
home where we would be blessed to have
all of the tools that could conceivably
be necessary to validate God's faith
in us; to see if we could muster an
equivalent faith in His Plan for
us, and in the infinite and
eternal Atonement
of His Son.

When we
have stockpiled
sufficient assets in
our spiritual savings
accounts, when they are
nearing their depletion, or
if our accounts are overdrawn,
the financial institution whose
reserves are found in The Book of
Mormon will distribute pennies
from heaven, or the currency
of faith, that takes on
myriad forms.

In The Book of Mormon,
every time that we encounter
the doctrine of the Atonement of
our Savior Jesus Christ, our sinews
will resonate with recognition. It is in
this way that we have all been blessed
with the innate capacity to hearken
to the voice of the Spirit, even to the
Light of Christ, that guides us to
the warm embrace of our Father,
Who will reach out to us from
heaven and draw us
to His bosom.

It's been argued by some, that our
society has paid a heavy price because it
lacks a faithful focus on the restoration of
the gospel together with the gift of The Book of
Mormon. For example, it seems that its spiritual
equilibrium has become disoriented and its moral
compass is spinning wildly out of control. That
would explain why its values appear to have
been hastily adjusted in an unconscious,
misguided, and vain attempt to regain
a state of balance between heaven
and earth.

Those who are lazy
in their gospel discipleship
and do not make their study of
The Book of Mormon a daily habit,
might well ask: "What do I want out of
life?" while those of faith inquire: "What
would God have me do?" At a basic level,
idleness is the devil's workshop, and so our
refusal to be up and doing in the wake of
the restoration of the gospel is sin. It is
wasting our precious opportunities for
renewal in fruitless pursuits when we
should have been engaged in other
and better activities for which we
have been blessed with God-
given capabilities.

By
allowing
ourselves to be
habitually distracted
by trifling concerns until
they become the center of our
attention and even our obsession,
we ignore our innate desire to exercise
our faith to believe in the heaven-sent
origins of The Book of Mormon, and
thereby we commit a grievous
sin of omission.

It is the
false gods of
secular humanism
and similar ideologies
that extoll the virtues of the
intellect and demand tangible
proof that destroy our faith in
Jesus Christ. As Alma taught
the Zoramites, they will divert
us from following a Plan whose
successful execution hinges
upon nourishing the seeds
of innocent faith in its
capacity to save us
from our sins.

A testimony
of the truthfulness of
the doctrine in The Book of
Mormon includes three essential
elements. Initially, we are introduced
to the principle, as we earnestly study the
scriptures that are related to it. Second, is
our correct understanding of the counsel
of the Lord concerning the principle,
that comes with illumination that
we receive from the Holy Ghost.
And lastly, is our experience
with the principle, which is
the fruits of faith. (See
Galatians 5:2).

The fabric of our faith in the divine origin of The Book of Mormon can be traced back to the spiritual swaddling clothes that have been integrated into our coats of many colors. It is a faith resonating with intrinsic light, betraying the fact that its vibrancy is due to more than just pigment and dye. It comes from the Holy Ghost.

Our study of The Book of Mormon leads to purposeful performance. It must involve a vital, personal commitment to practical belief. But at the end of the day, our good works lack the efficacy for salvation. Faith in the Savior of the world is what activates God's grace in our behalf, and it is that power alone that will save us, after all we can do.

When we stand before the pleasing bar
of God, the evidence will be presented, and our
previous conformity to or rejection of eternal law will
determine our reward or punishment. However, our innate
capacity to have generated faith in the divine origin of Book of
Mormon doctrine, due to the influences of the Light of Christ and the
Holy Ghost, has made our mortal experiences more than just a roll of the
dice. At the bar, we will finally understand that our lives hadn't been a
zero-sum game, after all. In fact, the cards had been marked and the
deck stacked in our favor. Life hadn't been a game of chance, but
rather an exercise involving skill. It was meant to be an exciting
adventure, overseen by God, for knowledge is power, which
renders the Judgment a win-win for both Him and
His children . (See Jacob 6:13 & Moroni 10:34).

We are not
ashamed to "declare
his doing among the people."
Without embarrassment, it's easy
"to make mention that His name is
exalted." (2 Nephi 22:4). We join with
our fellow Saints who have chosen to
"stand as witnesses of God at all
times and in all things, and
in all places ... even unto
death." (Mosiah
18:9).

When we
learn the language
of The Book of Mormon
(and especially of 2 Nephi
Chapters 12-24) we'll be blessed
with comprehension of a celestial
vernacular that is soothing to our
ears and calming to our souls. The
voice of the Spirit will be rhythmical
and melodious. As we hear it quietly
whisper: "You're a stranger here," it
will be comforting as we discover
that we "have wandered from
a more exalted sphere."
(Eliza R. Snow).

An investment
in the study of The
Book of Mormon provides
us with a handsome return,
and with currency sufficient
for our needs, but it also allows
us, if we so choose, to substitute its
legal tender for stacks of counterfeit
cash with which late payments may be
made, with interest and penalties tacked
on to our debt as a necessary consequence
of bad behavior. Under those circumstances,
it could even be that our lease on life would be
threatened with cancellation for nonpayment
of the charges and levies that accumulate as
we conduct the business of our lives in
the three-ring circus of commerce.

We can
enlarge the
foundations of
our spiritual center,
and we make room for
faith, even if the parts we
have been asked to play in
the drama of our lives seems
awkward. After we have signed
the papers, and we join other cast
members in the production of God's
Plan, we are reinvigorated to vividly
roleplay, to animatedly preplay, and
to repetitively replay the lines we have
been asked to deliver in the theater of
life. Rehearsals that are conducted by
the Spirit will give us courage to be
perfect in the delivery of our lines
and take our cues, with the goal
of delivering a performance
that is worthy of an
Oscar.

Alma taught his
brethren in Zarahemla
that it is our purpose in life
to grow in grace, that we might
progress in stature until we reach
the point that we have developed
both the image and likeness
of our Heavenly Father.
(See Alma 5:14).

Whenever we attempt to shirk the demands that the Spirit places upon us when we've been invited to try the virtue of the word of God, (see Alma 31:5), we risk being swallowed up by a leviathan that is no less real than the one that confronted Jonah. When that is the case, we must then resign ourselves to eventually be spit out upon the rocky shoreline of our doubts, fears, and apprehensions.

The Book of Mormon has extended a wonderful blessing to the faithful: Perfect repentance witnessed by the Spirit of Justification, that compels us to consider the possibility that, by the grace of God, we might one day actually be holy and without spot, as is our Lord and Savior.

The world seeks
change by exerting
external controls, and
fails miserably. The Book
of Mormon, however, takes
an innovative approach and
influences the inner vessel,
succeeding brilliantly by
recalibrating our internal
compass so that we might
remain oriented toward
the principles of the
gospel.

The raw and ugly soul scars that
are the festering residue of unresolved
sinful behavior are incompatible with the
uncompromising standard of prophylaxis or
spiritual hygiene that's been made possible
by the Atonement, and that is required
of those whose desire, one day, is to
inhabit the heavens, to live in the
company of both God and
angels. (See Alma
5:21).

Joseph
Smith might
have been referring
to The Book of Mormon,
when he declared: "This is good
doctrine. It tastes good. I can taste
the principles of eternal life, and so
can you. They are given to me by the
revelations of Jesus Christ; and I know
that … you believe them. I can taste the
spirit of eternal life. I know it is good,
and when I tell you of these things
which were given me by inspiration
of the Holy Spirit, you are bound
to receive them as sweet,
and rejoice."

When those who read
The Book of Mormon wrest the
scriptures, it captures our attention.
Those who do so will sometimes suggest
with a misinterpretation of the teachings
of the prophets that we are saved by works,
twisting holy writ from its true or proper
signification, and perverting it from
its correct application. Make no
mistake, however. We are
saved by the grace of
God, and by that
alone.

The
Book of Mormon
helps us to redefine
and redesign what had
heretofore been stumbling
blocks; they are repurposed
into the very stepping stones
that are needed to conquer our
fears, to bolster our confidence,
and to overcome the obstacles
that are strewn about all
along the path of our
progression.

Without
our Savior's spiritual
fitness program described in
The Book of Mormon and that
was designed to help us achieve
symmetry through repentance,
day-to-day life in the lone
and dreary world would
lack coherence and
stability.

We have
been converted to
The Book of Mormon
when we begin to hear it
calling to us, inviting us to
come in out of the cold and
out of the darkness into
the marvelous light
of day.

The
Book of Mormon
teaches all the world
that "this life is the time to
prepare to meet God, yea, behold
the day of this life is the day for
(us) to perform (our) labors," and to
initiate the process of healing the soul
scars of sin thru purposeful repentance,
and to attend to every needful thing in
anticipation of our resurrection to glory
and of a wonderful reunion that will
incude all of our loved ones in the
Celestial Kingdom of God.
(Alma 34:32).

With our Book of Mormon study, the righteousness of our efforts will be revealed in spectacular plainness and simplicity. Any walls of opposition that have been thrown up to block our purposeful and sincere inquiry will crumble and fall away. During our efforts, the Lord will comfort and succor us with the Bread of Life. As we journey through the harsh and unforgiving environment of Babylon, seeking the Lord while He may be found, oases will spring up in the deserts for living water to slake our thirst.

With the guidance provided by Book of Mormon prophets, it becomes easier to negotiate the strait and narrow path all the way to the Tree of Life, there to partake of its delicious fruit, which represents eternal life in the Celestial Kingdom of God.

The
principles
and doctrines of
The Book of Mormon
were the foundation of
our pre-mortal classroom
curriculum. The incentive
to initiate decisive action
rests with each one of us,
and it is the Spirit that
invites us to experience
religious recognition,
or the re-knowing
of what we have
beforehand
learned.

If we hope to be
able to successfully
deal with inequalities of
life and escape the quicksand
of self-pity, we must personalize
the lessons of The Book of Mormon.
That is best accomplished during the
hour of prayer that is found within
Sacrament meeting. Pondering the
Savior's forgiveness of our sins, we
visualize Him standing before the
golden gate of heaven, patiently
waiting for us to acknowledge
the transcendent beauty of
His power to transform
our lives.

Even as our ears are assaulted by sounding brass and tinkling cymbals, when we have tended our testimonies of The Book of Mormon, we'll find within ourselves the ability to sift thru the discordant cacophony of confusing voices to find rhythms of revealed truth and a harmonious balance between heaven and earth. Our craving to be clean will find an avenue for expression in celestial sparks that will ignite our desire to repent.

Every one of the laws of God has been perfectly crafted with His children in mind, to have both blessings and punishment affixed to it. Our obedience brings happiness, while disobedience always ends badly. "Despair cometh because of iniquity." (Moroni 10:22). That is the feeling of helplessness which is one of the natural consequences of the violation of the eternal laws that govern heaven.

Grace has power to raise us from physical death by the resurrection, and from spiritual death thru the Atonement of Christ. We receive the grace of God proportionately as we conform to His standard of personal righteousness that can only be found in the teachings of the gospel of Jesus Christ, and particularly within the pages of The Book of Mormon.

"I shall speak unto the Jews and they shall write it; and I shall also speak unto the Nephites and they shall write it; and I shall also speak unto the other tribes of the house of Israel, which I have led away, and they shall write it; and I shall also speak unto all nations of the earth and they shall write it." (2 Nephi 29:12).

Whenever the arm of the Lord is revealed, (see 2 Nephi 8:9) we can be certain of His mighty power - our sure source of strength and support. The arm of flesh, conversely, is unstable, and is prone to uncontrollable spasm, atrophy, and paralysis, that are all symptoms of clumsy outbursts of behavior that is destructive and ineffectual.

Heavenly Father is "mighty to save" (Alma 34:18) and is ready to forgive those who walk in darkness, and who know not where to find gospel truth. He is anxious to reach out to those who have helplessly endured the night and have suffered the pain of spiritual blindness.

A consuming fire
and billowing clouds of
smoke (see 2 Nephi 20:17)
as well as deeply penetrating
burnings, an ethereal light, and
a sharp and piercing spirit, are all
symbolic of the presence of the Lord,
and of the glory of God. Frequently,
they depict the splendor of celestial
realms. As Joseph Smith taught:
"God Himself dwells in
eternal fire."

The Book
of Mormon illustrates
our interesting relationship
with God as He brings to pass our
immortality and eternal life within
our biological broth whose secret spice is
unbridled free will. It is unthinkable that He
would focus His energies and concentrate His
power on an activity that was doomed to failure
because of flaws in the very instruments that were
critical to its success and were also the center of His
attention. The little boy who exclaimed: "God don't
make junk!" betrayed a keen wisdom beyond his
years. Victor Hugo may have heard the majestic
clockwork, when he wrote: "Be like a bird that
pausing in her flight a while on boughs to
light, feels them give way beneath her
and yet sings, knowing that
she has wings."

The
Book of Mormon
illustrates how life is
made up of endless chains
of spiritual experiences that
are balanced by the counterpoint
of worldliness. At first, there appears
to be a wide gulf between our spiritual
and temporal sides, that one would think
might make things easier for the righteous.
These contrasting sides of our nature seem
to be incompatible. But without a working
knowledge of the principles of the Plan, it
would be much more difficult to reconcile
the two and enjoy a state of holiness as
our natural habitat, richer for having
had our mortal experiences. We are
not to be worn down by life, or to
be overcome by evil influences,
but rather to be refined and
purified by adversity, by
danger, by misfortune,
by challenges, and
by contraries.

The
Book of Mormon
permits us to brush up
against the face of God. It
"gentles our condition,"
as Shakespeare's
King Henry V
would say.

Our rendezvous with the judgment won't come at some hazy point down the road. (See Mormon 7:6). It is happening today, and we speak, think, and act according to either celestial, terrestrial, or telestial law. We are blessed with a moral compass. Our faith in Christ, with its evidence in action, clearly defines the path that we have chosen to follow. Each day that we live, we are 24 hours closer to the Pleasing Bar of Christ. If we have committed the 13th Article of Faith to practice as well as to memory, its principles will have become the particles of our faith. We believe in being honest, true, chaste, benevolent, and in doing good to all men. Indeed, we may say that we follow the admonition of Paul. If there is anything virtuous, lovely, or of good report or praiseworthy, we seek after these things. (See Philippians 4:8).

The Book of Mormon is an extraordinary work, validating the supposition that there are rhythms in nature that we can feel only when we are in harmony with eternal principles.

Book of Mormon
prophets suggest that
we who have come to earth to
fight the battle that is raging in
the hearts of men on Saturday were
counted as the valiant in the pre-earth
existence, and that during the propaganda
war that was waged by Satan to gain control
of the minds of his brothers and sisters, we were
passionate in our defense of agency. (See 2 Nephi
24:12). Following that struggle, free will prevailed,
and when it was time for the victorious spirits to come
to the earth, they did so with a passion for their hard-won
freedom to choose their own destiny. Therefore, when those
spirits are now controlled by compulsion in any degree of
unrighteousness dominion, their ingrained tendency is
to resist. Therefore, we need to be very cautious when
interacting with our youth, when questions
arise that involve the exercise of their
divine right of free will.

Ralph Waldo Emerson
once observed: "If the stars
in heaven should appear but
one night in a thousand years,
how would men believe and adore,
and preserve for many generations,
the remembrance of the city of God
which had been revealed." In The Book
of Mormon, we read of such an event,
unprecedented in the history of the
world: "And it came to pass also
that a new star did appear,
according to the word."
(3 Nephi 1:21).

The Lord has admonished us to love our enemies, and to do good to them, and to lend, hoping for nothing again; and our reward shall be great. (See 3 Nephi 12:44 & Luke 6:35). The "get even" mentality of revenge that is so popularized in books and films and reinforced in everyday interpersonal relationships, in commerce, and social settings, is antithetical to the gospel of Jesus Christ. It may be that in business, you don't get what you deserve; you get what you negotiate. But when the earth has been cleansed to receive its paradisiacal glory, a much higher standard will prevail. Before that happens, the Saints have the responsibility to prepare the earth for the Millennium, when the lion and the lamb will lie down together in harmony.

The Nephites were drawn to Eastern mysticism just as moths are attracted to fire, and they were mesmerized by its worldly manifestations, even though it was only an illusion and a caricature of the awesome power that was symbolized by the burning bush. Sinai, after all is said, is an attitude more than it is a place. The faithful and true loose the latchets of their sandals because they realize that holy sanctuaries have been designed to be a part of their daily experience, and are ever before their face.

If we
ignore the
twin influences
of the Light of Christ
and the Holy Ghost that
nurture our innate yearning to
abhor mischief, but instead allow
ourselves to be habitually distracted
by trifling concerns, we sin by omission
and risk settling for life in a marshland
of mediocrity that quickly degenerates in
to a quicksand of sin, from which there
is no escape unless we take advantage
of the buoyancy that is provided by
the Atonement of Jesus Christ.
This is a repetitive message
that is found throughout
the pages of The Book
of Mormon.

The Book of Mormon introduces us to a
familiarity with principles that stands in sharp
contrast to the values of society that are continually
morphed by the shifting sands of cultural expediency.
The covenants we are encouraged to make by Book of
Mormon prophets protect us from these mutating
tenets, and provide a stable moral basis that
shapes us as we develop into the full
stature of our spirits.

Timorous and fragile souls who are cautiously hesitant and tentatively faithful don't consciously intend to lose the desire to seek truth. Their innocent faith simply fades away, like the slow leak in an automobile tire, and not as a blowout. But, it may often be traced back to the tendency to mischief that may have taken root during a time of particularly intense vulnerability to the wiles of the Devil.

Although it has been only briefly alluded to in The Book of Mormon (see Alma 46:23) Joseph's coat of many colors can serve as a metaphor for our faith in the Atonement of Jesus Christ. If we look closely at its fabric, it teaches us that even the most menacing clouds have silver linings, and we will realize that the bright dawning of a new day will follow on the heels of even the darkest of nights.

Thanks be unto our Heavenly Father for the penetrating clarity of the teachings of every Book of Mormon prophet, to help us get thru each day, and to comfort us during every long night of darkness. Truly, He will stay up late, and He leaves a light burning for us, to guide us back to our home.

There is nothing else on earth that can make up for the revelatory rewards that are such prominent features of The Book of Mormon. Cheap thrills won't replace its originality. Neither novelty nor spectacle can defeat, but can only delay, implementation of its principles. The universal influence of the Light of Christ encourages us to set our sights on the brightly burning beacon of the the Savior of the world, as well as on the Holy Ghost, Who is waiting to guide us, in the company of the God, angels, and witnesses, across an ocean of light to a new world that only awaits our discovery.

Lehi taught that without redemption from sin, if they were to have partaken of the fruit of the Tree of Life, which is eternal life, or the highest expression of the love of God, it would not have been possible for Adam and Eve to sustain a celestial existence, inasmuch as in their current condition they wouldn't have been capable of obedience to the laws that govern those who inherit the glory of heaven. (See 2 Nephi 2:25). Without the Atonement the Plan of Salvation would have been frustrated, not only for them, but also for all of the children of God who would follow after them.

Whenever we undertake a well-intentioned, purposeful and comprehensive examination of the Book of Mormon's merits, we are immediately struck by the realization that our spiritual awakening will progress only as long as we are learning. We take solace in the fact that, although we are admonished 154 times in the scriptures to be perfect, we are also encouraged 129 times to "learn" and 995 times to "begin."

The Day
of Judgment
does not lie over a
distant horizon, but is
today. We speak, think, and
act according to the celestial,
terrestrial, or telestial laws that
are before us. Just as a barometer
is used to measure the direction
in which the weather is headed,
The Book of Mormon helps us
to be aware of the bearing we
must take if we hope to
reach the shelter and
security of our
home port in
heaven.

The necessity
of the doctrine of
opposition (see 2 Nephi
2:10-13 & Alma 42:16)
does not give us license to
act recklessly or capitulate in
our behavior to the dark side, in
the mistaken belief that we will be
able to shift the blame and avoid
responsibility for our actions. The
Atonement stands at attention, to
replace the shattered vestiges of
our lives, and restore us to
our perfect and proper
frames, so that we
will be as good
as new.

No wind can
blow except it fills
our sails to carry each of
us closer to our destination,
in the direction of our destiny,
without any delay or interruption,
and without unnecessary cost, loss,
or sacrifice. All that is required of us to
gain a witness of The Book of Mormon is a
contrite spirit. We rely upon the power of the
Savior's gentle breeze to nudge our fragile
vessels onward upon the ocean of life, while
intermittent moments of calm seem to be
accompanied by the distant sound of
seafarer's shanties. These appear to
be the music of God's heavenly
choir, whose primary purpose
is to reinvigorate hearts
that are broken in
humility.

We learn
in The Book of Mormon
that following the ministry
of the Savior among the Nephites,
their love for Him, and for each other,
was so great that they were the happiest
people of all those who had ever been
created by the hand of God.
(See 4 Nephi 1:15-16).

Those
vacillating souls
of anemic will who give
up their freedom to choose in
exchange for the flavor of the day,
or for whatever provocative pleasures
their poor choices may provide, will be
snared by Satan and bound by his strong
chains. Only too late, they realize that it is their
misguided loyalties that have significantly
curtailed their ability to take advantage
of the gifts of The Book of Mormon,
that they might enjoy the perfect
law of liberty.

The
Book of Mormon
clearly describes how
we all have the capacity
to develop the nature of God.
(See Alma 41:2-6 & 13). After
all, we are His children. As any
reasonable parent would, He simply
asks us to obey His household rules. He
commands us to repent, to be baptized,
and to exercise faith in the power of the
Atonement to save us from our sins. He
gives us the gift of the Holy Ghost to
help us meet these requirements, so
that we might have a hope in our
Savior, that we might one day
gain readmittance to our
family household
of glory.

Habitual sin is a quicksand miring the unwary in mind-numbing conformity, a monotonously repetitive predictability, and in an underwhelming convention. (See Alma 41:10 & Mormon 2:13). These are the polar opposites of the imaginative spontaneity and the refreshingly distinctive artistic individuality that are among the blessings that we receive because of our acceptance of the truthfulness of Book of Mormon doctrine.

If the truth were to be told, it's only when we have enrolled in the graduate school of hard knocks, and have pre-paid the required tuition, that we'll obtain the credits that are to be earned by our strict obedience to the daunting curriculum of contrition. We learn to forgive others as Jesus Christ will forgive each of us our trespasses (see 3 Nephi 13:15) through His infinite and eternal Atonement for the sins of the world, from the beginning to the end of time.

When
Adam and
Eve were driven
from the Garden,
they were "punished"
with the very thing that
would later prove to bring
them the greatest happiness.
(See 2 Nephi 2:11). The Sufi
poet Rumi echoed Lehi, when he
wrote that our wounds become the
portals that allow light to enter us.
A Savior would be provided for God's
children, but in the interim, cherubim
and a flaming sword were set in place to
keep the way of the Tree of Life, to observe
the doctrines of Justice and of Mercy and
to initialize the principle of repentance
that is founded upon the doctrine of
the Atonement. In the Garden, after
their fall from grace, our first
parents were commanded
to have faith in all
these things.

Many forms
of poetry exist in The
Book of Mormon. In fact,
they pervade the text, and they
are often strategically placed in
order to highlight the importance of
particular passages. Even the Bard
of Avon would be impressed by
its grace and beauty.

The cataracts
that are created by our
concessions to sin cloud our
vision. Our narrow perspective
forces us into making comfortless
compromises, leaving the landscapes
of our lives as nothing more than empty
shells. If we do not take advantage of the
therapy of repentance thru the Atonement
of Jesus Christ, that is encouraged by every
Book of Mormon prophet, the prognosis for
success is poor for eyes that have lost the
ability to see clearly, and that can no
longer make the distinctions between
good and evil, between light and
darkness, between pleasure
and pain, and between
virtue and vice.

Our love
of the scriptures,
and particularly of The
Book of Mormon, has been
nurtured within our spiritual
kindergarten. It is heightened in
our mortal classroom, and it will
be established in eternity, when
heaven will smile upon us and
we will be clothed in the
glory of God.

Nothing
short of sin will
motivate us to drag
our battered and beaten
bodies to the gym that goes
by the moniker of The Church of
Jesus Christ of Latter-day Saints.
For it is there, under the direction and
guidance of priesthood fitness trainers,
that we're encouraged to participate in the
robust spiritual workouts that introduce us
to their prominent regimens. These include
an easy familiarity with the mission of the
Prophet Joseph Smith, a testimony of The
Book of Mormon, and most important
of all, a relationship with our
Savior Jesus Christ.

Our eternal focus
of faith is nurtured when
we "discard the poor lenses of
our bodies, and are able to peer
thru a telescope of truth into the
infinite reaches of immortality."
(Helen Keller). But if we turn our
backs on the invitation to have a
relationship with God through The
Book of Mormon, and we remain
alienated from Him by spiritual
death, we will be forced by the
Adversary to surrender our
fortunes to inclinations
that are carnal and
sensual.

We think of Abinadi, when we read about Joan of Arc, who stood before the stake, and was offered her freedom by denying what she believed. Instead, she declared: "Every man and woman gives their lives for what they believe. Sometimes, when people believe in little or nothing, they give their lives for little or nothing. One life is all we have, and we live it as we believe in living it, and then it is gone. But to surrender what you are, and to live without belief, is more terrible than dying. It is even more terrible than dying young."

Wresting the holy scriptures, and suggesting that we are saved by our own works, twists holy writ from its true or proper signification, and perverts it from its correct or its rightful application. Lest we deceive ourselves, let it be known that we all need the clarity of Book of Mormon teachings, if we wish to be saved in the Kingdom of God.

As active
cast members in
life's Three Act Play,
we can better understand
our roles if we have engaged
others in the scenes we play. We
need to be on familiar terms with
those who participate in the drama,
and share the stage with them as we
rehearse, thru our study of The Book
of Mormon, the challenges we face
that are related to mastering the
assignments that are, in turn,
attached to each of our
individual parts.

"The ancient
record thus brought
forth out of the earth as
the voice of a people speaking
from the dust, and translated
into modern speech by the gift
and power of God as attested by
Divine affirmation, was first
published to the world in the
year 1830 as The Book of
Mormon." (Testimony
of the Prophet Joseph
Smith).

Alma
taught that,
in the absence of
their repentance for
their sins, and without
the benefit of covenants,
Adam and Eve would have
ultimately been miserable.
(See Alma 42:11 & 12:26).
To be sure, they would have
lived forever, but without
the Atonement, it would
have been in a state of
perpetual alienation
from the hearth
and home of
God.

When
the Nephites
were righteous, they
seldom forgot to call upon
God to protect them from worldly
influences, and from that old serpent
Beelzebub. They were acutely aware that
Satan was abroad in the land, for they had
often heard, and sometimes responded to,
his siren call coming from Babylon,
that rang loudly in their ears,
even as they sang "the
song of redeeming
love." (Alma
5:26).

Our Father Who dwells
in Heaven never envisioned that
our testimonies of The Book of Mormon
would follow the receipt of signs from above.
Our faith precedes the miracle. We must take a few
steps into the darkness before the flaming fire of the
Spirit will illuminate the way that lies before us. A
confirmation by the Holy Ghost will always flow
along the pathway that has been created by
faith, even if it passes uncomfortably
close to great and spacious
buildings.

Baptism
catalyzes both the
temporal and spiritual
execution of God's Plan. Our
baptismal covenant allows us to
continually monitor our relationship
with Him during our engagement with
mortality. Our salvation hinges upon our
correct understanding of the points of
doctrine that focus on our salvation,
and that are clearly illustrated
in The Book of Mormon.

We are
familiarized
thru The Book of
Mormon to the Holy
Ghost, Who is the author
of our acumen, the avatar
of our agency, the architect
of our aptitude, the benefactor of
all of our blessings, the designer of
discipleship, the initiator of insight,
the inventor of intelligence, the patron
of perception, the provider of our praise,
the sponsor of our scholarship, and the
ultimate source of our understanding;
not to mention the craftsman of our
comfort, the guarantor of all gifts,
and the champion of committed
Christians everywhere.

Nearly every time disobedient Nephites turned their
backs on the Law, no matter the magnitude of their
temporal preparation, it proved to be of no benefit in
avoiding the pitfalls to their progression, with the
inevitable consequence that disaster then rained
down upon their society. That calamity has
been symbolized in the scriptures by the
burning of stubble and of chaff that
are very quickly engulfed,
and then consumed
by fire.

The Book
of Mormon
will expose us to
opportunities to bear
each other's burdens. It
does not debate the merits
of the petitions of the weak
and impoverished who need
our aid and it turns a blind
eye to our prejudices that
threaten to influence the
depth and breadth of
our compassion.

The Book of
Mormon reestablishes
the precise synchronicity
that should exist between the
daily demands that we all face
during mortality and the grand
scope of the divine design of our
Heavenly Father. It conforms to
a majestic clockwork that was
calibrated at the creation of
the world to coordinate
with heaven's time
frame.

By reading in The Book of Mormon about the account of the ideological War in Heaven, we know that a 'third part' of the children of our Heavenly Father forfeit their privilege to obtain a body. (See 2 Nephi 24:12-16). For those who remained faithful, however, there came humbling liabilities, for The Plan required the Creator to die for our sins to mercifully satisfy the demands of Justice, in an act of Atonement that would be conditional only upon our repentance.

The day-to-day 'nuts and bolts' elements of the Plan are put in perspective by The Book of Mormon, so that we might more clearly distinguish the grey-toned obstacles that lie in our path. These barriers to our progression will then stand out in sharp contrast against the polychromatic backdrop of the design that God has created through the sacrifice of our Savior, Jesus Christ.

The tree of life represents the love of God. The fruit of this tree, as expected, represents eternal life, which is the greatest gift our Father could give His children. There are many who are actively, passionately, and desperately fighting their way through swirling mists of darkness toward the tree of life and its precious fruit. In Nephi's account, when they finally arrive at the tree, they'll fall down completely spent and exhausted for their efforts. New meaning is given to the apostle Paul's admonition that we ought to work out our own salvation with fear and trembling before the Lord. (See Philippians 2:12).

Nothing short of sin will motivate us to drag our battered and beaten bodies to the gym that goes by the moniker of The Church of Jesus Christ of Latter-day Saints. For it is there, under the direction and guidance of priesthood fitness trainers, that we're encouraged to participate in the robust spiritual workouts that introduce us to their prominent regimens. These include an easy familiarity with the mission of the Prophet Joseph Smith, a testimony of The Book of Mormon, and most important of all, a relationship with our Savior Jesus Christ.

When Laman, Lemuel, Sam, and Nephi returned to Jerusalem to obtain the Plates of Brass from Laban, they first went back to their home on the outskirts of the city, and gathered up all the treasures they had left behind. These they took to the house of Laban, and offered them in exchange for what they really considered precious. But the Lord did not allow them to receive the spiritual gift of the scriptures in exchange for the profane baubles and ornaments of the world. Ultimately, at the hands of their unscrupulous cousin, they lost these telestial trinkets so that the Lord might thereafter prove to them that He was mightier than man, saw the end from the beginning, and was firmly in control of both their temporal and their spiritual destiny.

One thing we learn from excitedly reading about the contraries of the Nephites and Lamanites in The Book of Mormon is that some people are defined by their temporal trappings that distract them from the intangible substance that can be found at the core of their existence, while others have woven ecclesiastical embroidery into the coat of many colors that should be a foundation garment of their heavenly wardrobe. These may consist of doctrinal decorations or improvised accouterments that are designed to prop up their faltering faith. Self-actualized members of the church, however, take their cues from the inside. The source of their real power lies in dreams, ideals, values, and core operating principles. These are not easily subject to change, and are not readily affected by outside influences. Their healthy reliance upon the tender mercies of Christ provides just the balance they need, and gives them a vision of their potential to become self-directed, self-managed, and self-motivated, all within the context of God's Plan.

We are enveloped in light. (See Mosiah 16:9). When the Nephites were at their best, they did as Helen Keller suggested, when she said: "Keep your face to the sunshine, and you can't see the shadow." The shadow will still exist, but if we are oriented toward the light, it will always be behind us, out of sight, and out of mind. Light can be the catalyst that transforms timidity and temerity into powerful presence of mind, which then acts as a platform for assertive action. It is not bravado, but boldness. It is an intense and compellingly positive response to challenge. In the fight or flight scenario, it is the launching pad for the anticipated adrenalin rush that carries us beyond the threat. It is the foundation quality upon which is built our nobility.

The Nephites always paid a hefty price for their lack of vision. Whenever their culture lost its spiritual equilibrium, too often, it simply adjusted its values in a realignment with worldly coordinates. We can be sure that it justified its worship of gods of wood and stone as multi-culturalism. It embraced perversion, and legitimized it as an alternative lifestyle. The poor were exploited in the name of government lotteries. When unborn children were killed, the collective conscience was soothed by calling it pro-choice. Power was abused and it was dismissed as "politics." If obscenities polluted the media, it would have been characterized as the freedom of expression. The target had been moved so many times, that they thought they were scoring repetitive bulls-eyes, when in reality, they were far from the mark.

It was in the Fifth Century
A.D., at the commencement of the
Middle Ages that the White Martyrs
of Christian Ireland clothed themselves
in distinctive white wool robes and fanned
out all across Europe. In dozens of locations,
they founded monasteries. Their influence is
incalculable. They re-established literacy, and
breathed new life into the exhausted cultures
of Europe. "And that is how the Irish saved
civilization." (Thomas Cahill). P.S. And
that is also how the Sons of Mosiah
saved the Anti-Nephi-Lehies.
(See Alma 23:5-8).

In language that is peculiar, or unique,
to The Book of Mormon, the prophet-historian
Mormon recorded that Jesus "smile(d) upon them
and behold, they were as white as the countenance and
also the garments of Jesus; and behold the whiteness thereof
did exceed all the whiteness, yea, even there could be nothing
upon earth so white as the whiteness thereof." (3 Nephi 19:25).
They had been purified thru the redeeming blood of Christ,
and by the grace of God they were saved. They enjoyed a
relationship of the Second Comforter, and their faces
reflected His light. To the Latter-day Saints, the
Lord re-affirmed: "If your eye be single to
my glory, your whole bodies shall be
filled with light, and there shall
be no darkness in you."
(D&C 88:67).

Book of Mormon doctrine reaffirms that the highest pinnacle of spirituality is not joy in the unbroken sunshine, but absolute and undoubting trust in the love of God. Every life must endure a soaking rain every now and again, together with the attendant mud that inevitably follows. Change will come "like a clap of thunder, and a flash of lightning. But after the storm, flowers will bloom."
(I Ching).

Adversity can behave as a diamond dust that polishes us to a high luster, or it can be an abrasive that wears us down and grinds us up. However, we cannot hope to successfully deal with our difficulties without having first centered our lives on Jesus Christ. He said: "And if men come unto me, I will show unto them their weakness. I give unto men weakness that they may be humble; and my grace is sufficient for all men that humble themselves before me; for if they humble themselves before me, and have faith in me, then will I make weak things strong unto them."
(Ether 12:27).

The
righteous Nephites
seldom forgot to call upon
God to protect them from worldly
influences, and from that old serpent
Beelzebub. They were acutely aware that
Satan was abroad in the land, for they had
often heard, and sometimes responded to,
his siren call coming from Babylon,
that rang loudly in their ears,
even as they sang "the
song of redeeming
love." (Alma
5:26).

In addition to the
obvious reference to the
plates deposited at the Hill
Cumorah, "out of the ground"
and "low out of the dust" could
also refer to ancient records of lost
civilizations known only to God. Of
one such empire of antiquity, an Israeli
archaeologist who oversaw the excavation
of Masada observed: "Nothing remains
here today of the Romans, but a heap
of stones in the desert."
(Yigal Yadin).

The teachable Lamanites who were converted by the power of the preaching of the word by The Sons of Mosiah came out of the world and left the loneliness of a fallen creation to enter the realm of divine experience. They had forsaken the orphanage of spiritual alienation, and were welcomed into the household of God. Today, we do the same thing. We leave the ranks of the nameless and take upon ourselves another name, that of Jesus Christ, becoming, in time, joint-heirs of all that our Father has.

Employing rhetoric that sounds as if it could have been lifted out of the pages of The Book of Mormon, Abraham Lincoln declared: "It is the duty of men as well as nations to owe their dependence upon the over-ruling power of God, to confess their sins and transgressions in humble sorrow. Yet, with assured hope that genuine repentance will lead to mercy and pardon, (we must) recognize that those nations only are blessed, whose God is the Lord."

As we continue
our spiritual education,
The Book of Mormon will help
us to expand our spiritual capacity,
and to see as God sees, and to know and
understand as He does. When we turn our
attention to the interesting phrase "and thus
we see," that is used by the prophets, and to
its related variants, we open our minds
to pearls of great price and hidden
treasures of knowledge.

At Cumorah, Mormon
attempted to prick the hearts of
his people with the word, continually
stirring them up to purposeful repentance.
He felt it was his responsibility to heal their
deafness and blindness by applying a healing
balm to their spiritual muscles and joints. But it
was to no avail. He wrote to Moroni: "I am laboring
with them continually, and when I speak the word
of God with sharpness, they tremble and anger
against me; and when I use no sharpness they
harden their hearts against it, wherefore I
fear, lest the Spirit of the Lord hath
ceased striving with them."
(Moroni 9:4).

During what
can sometimes be
a long process of the
development of our faith
in The Book of Mormon, it
will become necessary for us to
take a few steps into the darkness
in order to allow the spiritual strong
searchlight of truth to illuminate the
way before us. Only after the trial of
our faith, will it be confirmed by the
Spirit that the book is everything
that its authors, and our Lord
and Savior, claim it to be.
(See D&C 17:6).

Every discussion of our faith in the
divine design elements of the Plan of our
Heavenly Father must distinguish it from
its caricatures. Our dialogue requires neither
naiveté, nor gullibility, nor wishful thinking.
While it demands more than confidence, it is
somehow greater than optimism. Our faith in
The Book of Mormon, for example, is not just
an exercise in positive thinking, and it is
far more than attitude. Saving faith
can move mountains, or at least
show us the way to climb over
our obstacles or to walk
around them.

It may seem
that the easier way
out is to adopt the ways
of the world. It may be harder
to acknowledge that there exists
with each of us an autobiographical
thread that leads all the way back to
heaven. Sometimes, we forget how The
Book of Mormon has been designed
to transform us, through the Plan
of Salvation, into a fine-tuned
and well-oiled machine for
the making of gods.

The Book of
Mormon functions
like a stethoscope with
the astonishing ability to
detect the vital capacity of
our spirit. When our hearts
have broken in contrition,
we are able to quantify the
steady sinus rhythm that
confirms the congruence
that must exist between
our terrestrial world
and the abode of
the gods.

While repentance is like
an inexhaustible fossil fuel
that fires our desire to follow in
the footsteps of the Lord, it is The
Book of Mormon that charges our
spiritual batteries, energizing our
sight and electrifying our vision
with infinite perspective. With
an awakening awareness, we
realize we can become holy
and without spot, thanks
to our Lord's sacrifice
in our behalf.

It is Satan's
Golden Question that
has always been "Do you
have any money?" He would
have us believe that we can have
anything in the world, for money.
Does a need exist? Solve the problem
with generous applications of money,
repeated in equal doses four times each
day for life. This is the prescription upon
which the world relies, shifting the blame
for their problems in a frantic flight from
accountability. It was always the plentiful
"gold and silver" of the Nephites that led to
their downfall. (See Alma 4:6). Babylon
has always clamored for an undeserved
entitlement, even as Zion embraces the
work ethic. Babylon always exhibits a
juvenile irresponsibility, whereas
Zion demonstrates spiritual
restraint and maturity.

However we fit into the grand scheme of the cosmos, we do know this: God quickens life by providing the animation of a physical world within which we freely interact; He "lends (us) breath, that (we) may live and move and do according to (our) own will, and (He supports us) from one moment to another." (Mosiah 2:21).

It's The Book of Mormon that generates repetitive opportunities to smell the delicious aroma of the bread of life that has been baking in a celestial oven. In anticipation of a buttered slice, we steadily move along upon the path that carries us closer to the window sill of the kitchen in our heavenly home.

As a bright beacon of hope twinkling hopefully and steadily in the night sky, the Church of Jesus Christ in the New World became a third class of witnesses to the birth of the Savior, joining the Wise Men and the shepherds in their fields. As a result, His people in Zarahemla began "to have peace in the land. And there were no contentions." (3 Nephi 1:23-24). The star in the East was symbolic of their focus on the Savior. His gospel was their fortification, obedience to their covenants was their sanctuary, and reliance upon the light was their protection against the prince of darkness, whose murky influence would soon enough be sweeping across the land like a suffocating wind.

Every day, we are 24 hours closer to the Pleasing Bar of Christ (Moroni 10:34) if we have patterned our lives after the 13th Article of Faith. We strive to "be honest, true, chaste, virtuous, and in doing good to all men. Indeed, we may say that we follow the admonition of Paul: We believe all things, we hope all things, we have endured many things, and hope to be able to endure all things. If there is anything that is virtuous, lovely, or of good report or praiseworthy, we seek after these things." In fact, "at the banquet of consequences, there will not be much that is satisfying at the table, unless we are able to bow our heads in reverence, not hang them in shame, in the presence of God, who will be there. " (Marion D. Hanks).

The
difficult
decision made
by Adam and Eve
in the Garden to choose
the harder right instead of
the easier wrong, obviated the
'Progression Paradox' that had
faced them, wherein they would
have remained forever in "a state
of innocence, having no joy, for
they knew no misery; doing no
good, for they knew no sin."
(2 Nephi 2:23). Their choice,
however, was anticipated
by the Atonement of
Jesus Christ.

People think
that they can be
happy if they wander
and play, forgetting that
a key feature of the Plan is
to ponder and pray, as Moroni
beseeched in Moroni 10:3. Only
then will they have the necessary
tools to find the happiness that's
been prepared for the Saints
in the household of
faith.

In The Book
of Mormon, we are
subjected to a constant
flow of insight, intuition,
inspiration, and revelation
that simply streams forth in
a downpour of divine direction
blessing us as we walk along
illuminated pathways and we
exercise our faculties of mind
and spirit. The book leads us
to the community where we
are no longer as strangers
or foreigners, but instead
are fellowcitizens with
the Saints, and with
the household of
God.

Even when
we believe that we have
fully committed ourselves to
the gospel of Jesus Christ, it will be
nothing short of regularly recurring
repentance, encouraged throughout The
Book of Mormon, that will provide us with
repetitive moments of confirmation; when
we will be blessed to say, as did those in
Zarahemla, that through the miracle
of forgiveness, by the power of the
Atonement and the grace of God,
our hearts have again been
changed thru faith on
the name of Jesus
Christ.

The Book of
Mormon teaches that
the Atonement of Christ
has such power that even if
we've been gravely wounded
by our sins, they will not heal
imperfectly, leaving soul scars.
Thru the application of the Balm
of Gilead, adhesions that have
been left behind by telestial
trauma will fade away,
until all evidence of
damage has been
erased.

It seems that whenever the lives of the Nephites were going
well, they were fooled into thinking that they could control events
and determine outcomes, when, in fact, most were beyond the vale of
their influence. What they could control was their creative and adaptive
response to the unpredictable circumstances that were a part of their daily
lives. They would not then be as children who had been tossed to and fro,
as flotsam and jetsam on the sea of life, and who were "carried about with
every wind of doctrine, by the sleight of men, and cunning craftiness."
(Ephesians 4:14). Today, there are those living among us who stand
for nothing but will fall for anything, and who think very
little of cursing the darkness without ever stopping to
light a candle. They lack a strong will, but make
up for it with an even more powerful won't.
If they bend their knee, they only do
so because they think they
are taking a bow.

Throughout The Book of Mormon, the Lord gives us repeated reassurance that it is His hand that will rule in the Last Days, and so His people need not fear the vile threats and dreadful oaths of the wicked. He has promised: "I will make thy horn iron, and I will make thy hoofs brass. And thou shalt beat in pieces many people; and I will consecrate their gain unto the Lord, and their substance unto the Lord of the whole earth." (3 Nephi 20:19).

Jacob warned those who had become preoccupied with telestial trivia: "Wo unto him ..... that wasteth the days of his probation, for awful is his state!" (2 Nephi 9:27). Particularly when individuals groan "under darkness and under the bondage of sin," they have little meaning or stability in their lives. (D&C 84:49). They do not understand that "fame is a vapor, and popularity is an accident, and that those who cheer you today may curse you tomorrow. In the end, the only thing that endures is character." (Anonymous).

We have seen that in Book of Mormon times, Ignorance was at the root of apostasy from the truth. Even today, the church suffers from a shallow understanding by many of its members of even basic gospel principles. Consequently, the devil seizes upon their weaknesses. Satan knows who the Lord's servants are; they are all marked men and women. Therefore, they require for a defense a solid foundation of doctrinal understanding, and a firm and abiding testimony of the principles of the Plan of Salvation and of the Savior.

Nephites "are like artichokes. At first, you either like them or you don't. But those who have had unfavorable first impressions quite often find that once the outer layers have been peeled away, both (Nephites) and artichokes are most likable. In fact, most people who get to know (Nephites) become their friends, while a little objective research on their beliefs reveals that, except for a few doctrinal differences, those who call themselves (the children of Lehi) are just like the rest of us. They are very human beings." ("Boston Globe," 1967).

If The Book of Mormon teaches us but little
else, it leaves us with this impression: Each of us
will find an opportunity to become familiar with the
principles of the Plan of Salvation, because, in the final
analysis, we cannot hope to find lasting happiness, except
we are obedient to the specific rules of behavior with which it is
associated. As Joseph Smith taught: "Happiness is the object and
design of our existence, and will be the end thereof, if we pursue
the path that leads to it, and this path is virtue, uprightness,
faithfulness, holiness, and keeping the commandments."
All else is vanity, and for the those of us who have been
exposed to The Book of Mormon, and who should
know better, it is blasphemous to act in
ways that are incompatible with
celestial principles.

Every time, in the final step
of their cyclical stages of righteousness,
prosperity, pride, and apostasy, and Nephites
found it within themselves to cultivate the quality
of contrition, good outweighed evil, love overpowered
jealousy, hate, and prejudice, light drove out darkness,
knowledge banished ignorance, humility displaced pride,
courtesy overwhelmed rudeness, and appreciation overcame
thanklessness. Abundance superseded poverty, well-being
replaced weakness, simplicity overshadowed perplexity, and
harmony supplanted discord. Faith subdued fear, a hope
in Christ cast out despair, charity ousted selfishness,
joy deposed unhappiness, sadness, dejection, and
misery, certainty dethroned bewilderment, and
confidence was substituted for timidity,
while assurance unseated despair
and discouragement.

The terrible indictment of those who have dismissed The Book of Mormon in the Last Days is that they will have little claim on mercy because they have willfully chosen to deny themselves the blessing of baptism by immersion for the remission of sins. For them, the judgment will be a very unpleasant experience, as an awful avalanche of consequences overwhelms them and smothers their hope of timely deliverance. Given over to the buffetings of Satan, on their own initiative they will somehow need to scrape together their last farthings in order to personally pay Justice, that they might meet its demands for their redemption.

The worth of principles is validated by our witness, or our testimony. The Book of Mormon emphasizes that baptism is the outward expression of our personal dedication to obedience. It is the public manifestation of our desire to have a private covenant relationship with God. It is the voluntary surrender of our agency to a higher power, the subjugation of our desires to His will.

Of one thing, Moroni had absolutely no doubt: That latter-day Israel would be brought of captivity and obscurity and gathered to the lands of her inheritance as well as to an awareness that the Lord Jesus Christ was her Redeemer. (See Moroni 10:31). The followers of Satan don't understand that, particularly in the Last Days, it is the arm of the Lord that is our real source of strength and support, in contrast to the arm of flesh which is unstable, volatile, and subject to senseless outbursts of violence.

There is a clear and unambiguous choice that every child of God has been blessed to make in this life, regardless of their circumstances. It doesn't matter if they are Jews or Gentiles, Nephites or Lamanites, Muslim or Christian, or believers or heathen. The choice is not between poverty and wealth, nor is it between sickness and health, or happiness and misery, or between fame and obscurity The choice is between good and evil. And so, when Jesus comes again, His glory will be like a fire that purges from blemished lives all of their accumulated impurities. Following the process of refining, if imperfections remain, a metal is without value. Good for nothing, it must be cast upon the scrap heap. Only if it has been cleaned of contamination, can it be fashioned into something of worth that will stand up under punishing use and give years of consistently reliable service.

"Isles of the sea" is a Semitic idiom that reflects the practice of sailing off to distant locations throughout the world. (See 1 Nephi 19:16, 21:8, 22:4, 2 Nephi 10:2 & 29:7). The continents of Asia and Africa, by contrast, were "the earth" because they had access to them by land. Idioms are expressions that are peculiar to a given culture, and we would expect Semitic examples throughout The Book of Mormon. The ease with which idioms have been sprinkled into the narrative suggests that they were utilized by Israelite authors. It begs our credulity to think that Joseph Smith could have been clever enough to employ them on his own and in perfect context.

Alma described God's divine design as the Plan of Salvation and of Redemption, Mercy, and Happiness, because it has made possible the resurrection of otherwise imperfect mortals to an eternal life of joy and glory. These "great and eternal purposes were prepared from the foundation of the world." (Alma 42:26). "To the Son is given the power of the resurrection, the power of the redemption, the power of salvation, the power to enact laws for the carrying out and accomplishment of the design. Hence, life and immortality are brought to light, the gospel is introduced, and He becomes the Author of eternal life and exaltation." (John Taylor).

The psalmist wrote: "But as for me ..... my clothing was sackcloth: I humbled my soul with fasting." (Psalms 35:13). This is good counsel that the Nephites would have been well to have taken from the Plates of Brass. When the law is written upon our hearts, and we feel the forgiveness of God, we must seize the opportunity at that very moment to forgive others, focusing spiritual power on our efforts, precisely because it is so contrary to our human nature to do so. (See 3 Nephi 12:44). The opportunity to forgive should never be wasted, because it awakens within our hearts spiritual sensitivity that is greater than ourselves. Brigham Young told the Saints that "he who takes offense when no offense was intended is a fool, and he who takes offense when it was intended is usually a fool."

The Book of Mormon illustrates that we are all influenced by Satan's bribes. But it is precisely because the Plan requires opposition that the earth has become an astonishing learning laboratory, a majestic clockwork, and a perfect 'machine for the making of Gods'. (Henri Bergson). But without the principles, the ordinances, and the covenants of the gospel that are designed to hold evil in check, mortality would've become nothing more than a malicious trap or a snare of Satan; and if he were to be given free-reign to attack the fold, his ravenous wolves would first scatter, then isolate, and finally devour at will every member of the flock of the Good Shepherd. Thank God, or hallelujah, for the community of the faithful!

Nephite (and Lamanite) prophets provided their people with celestial sign posts to guide them thru the telestial traffic jams that threatened to detour them from the strait and narrow way. At the same time, widening circles of opportunity were made accessible by obedience to gospel principles, assuring them that they would have direct exposure to the law of liberty. Thereby, they abandoned the tortuous route thru Idumea that was being taken by Lamanites who were bound for telestial glory. Instead, the righteous descendants of Lehi followed the unmistakable track that led to celestial surety in a heavenly setting.

"You ought to ask Mr. Mephistopheles, the original conjuring cat. The greatest magicians have something to learn from Mr. Mephistopheles' conjuring turn. And you'll all say: Oh! Well I never! Was there ever a cat so clever as magical Mr. Mephistopheles?" Mephistopheles, the prince of the power of the air, is a roaring lion, the angel of the bottomless pit, and a ruler of darkness. He was always probing Nephite defenses for signs of weakness in the fortress of their spiritual security. When they finally capitulated to his wiles and became entrenched in the habit pattern of sin, they felt uncomfortable associating with the more righteous members of their communities. At the same time, as they spiraled downward into the abyss of apostasy, their free will and power to change slipped away. The gates of hell loomed large, and the weight of the chains of Satan became oppressive for them to bear.

Untested potential is antithetical to the principles of God's great Plan of Salvation, for as the Lord said: "I will try the faith of my people." (3 Nephi 26:11). The Book of Mormon has been given to the world that it might be a part of that self-administered examination. The Saints are compelled to read it in order to nurture independent testimonies of its divine authenticity. If they do not wholeheartedly embrace the doctrine of Christ contained therein, and if they fail to live up to their covenants, they will be in the power of Satan. The inquisition that accompanied the grand experiment posited by Alma to the poor Zoramites portends an ominous consequence. None of us will receive an independent witness until after the trial of our faith. Only after we have passed through the refiner's fire will we be as tempered steel in our devotion to the Savior. "I have refined thee," said the Lord, "but not with silver; I have chosen thee in the furnace of affliction." (Isaiah 48:10).

When Lamanite ruffians came to scatter the flocks of King Lamoni, Ammon had unbridled confidence in the power of God. Therefore, he anticipated with joy a situation that, at the same time, must have caused palpitations in the hearts of his fearful companions. Today, we too must face our own "Lamanites by the Waters of Sebus." All of us have similar needs, but the primary focus of our shared concern should be on the preservation of our eternal lives. In truth, proper prior preparation, and abiding confidence in God's power, will prevent the poor performance of our priesthood-driven profession in the very hours of our greatest need.

We share the Good News
in a hierarchy that is initially based
on understanding, next on acceptance, then
on commitment, and finally on recommitment.
Our preaching is akin to understanding, teaching to
acceptance, expounding to commitment, and exhortation
to re-commitment. Our testimonies are expression of action
that follow the internalization of principles. They are borne with
strenuous effort that reflects the price we have paid to understand
the voice of the Lord concerning those principles. Testimony is a
reflection of the value that we place on direct experience with the
Spirit as it teaches us about those principles. Testimony isn't
free, but is purchased at a considerable expense. Testimony
releases the power of principles and empowers us to bind
ourselves to those principles by covenants of action
that increase our strength and endurance as
we learn to rely upon the Lord in all that
we say and everything that we do.
He completes us. He is both the
Author and the Finisher
of our faith.

One of the
basic messages of
The Book of Mormon
is that Adam and Eve
fell that they might have
joy during mortality and
in heaven, thru repentance
that had been activated by
their faith in the power of
the Atonement to save
them from, and not
in, their sins.

One of the greatest blessings that we can
receive from our Father in Heaven as we devour
The Book of Mormon is that when we internalize its
teachings "all the petty trials, sorrows, and sufferings of
life will fade away as temporary, harmless visions seen in a
dream." (David O. McKay). Our reverence for the Savior will
move beyond an association with the profane. Our standard
of reverence will be so high that we will have a desire to be
defenders of the faith when the line is crossed by those
who find fault with the principles of the gospel or the
Author of Salvation. As the Sons of Mosiah,
we will never hesitate to venture out of
the fold to rescue the lost sheep
who cross our paths.

The experiences that we have in mortality are the
active ingredients within a fertile matrix that has been
carefully prepared by our Father to vitalize the personalized
petri dish that is best suited to our individual circumstances.
This rich culture medium will become just the agar we need in
order to nurture our metamorphosis, to be transformed not by
maturation but by generation into the full stature of our
spirits. The infusion of a heavenly element readies
us to receive with equanimity whatever might
come during an incubation process that
was initiated by divine design
to be equally challenging
and rewarding.

When they unexpectedly find themselves bathed in the stunning clarity of light, those who are reading The Book of Mormon for the first time will often stare in wide-eyed wonder at the simplicity of the interwoven threads found within the pattern of gospel principles that make up the tapestry of the Plan of Salvation.

When we accept The Book of Mormon as holy scripture, we choose liberty and eternal life, instead of captivity and spiritual death. We choose to live our lives in accordance with the laws of the gospel. Without these laws, our unbridled freedom to choose might lead to tyranny. We are free to choose whether or not we wish to embrace the book, but we cannot choose to escape the consequences, if we choose unwisely.

It was at the
very instant when their
unsatisfied craving for the praise
and the popularity of the world began to
sway their behavior that the Nephites found
themselves in the uncomfortable position of
bending their character, when they thought
they were only taking a bow. It was chiefly
at this time that they needed the soothing
inspiration of the Holy Spirit, and the
healing guidance of their Lord and
Savior Jesus Christ, and finally
the nurturing encouragement
of their Father, Who looked
down upon them every
day of their lives,
from heaven
above.

It is the gospel of Jesus
Christ as it has been revealed in
The Book of Mormon that inspires us
to enthusiasm. After all, it is the good
news that practically begs us to experience
the feeling of being possessed by a god, to
have supernatural inspiration, and enjoy
prophetic frenzy. The definition found
in the dictionary is unmistakable. If
we are suffused with enthusiasm,
our actions are no longer ours;
for it is God Who has taken
control of our destiny,
with kindness and
benevolence.

The conduit to the living water that
is found in The Book of Mormon is created
when we not only believe, but we also act on our
belief, by being honest, true, chaste, benevolent,
virtuous, kind, and in doing good to others.
Living water has the power to sustain our
lives when we are doers, and not
only hearers, of the word.
(See James 1:22).

As we feast
upon the word of Christ
in The Book of Mormon, we
will receive health in our navels and
marrow in our bones, (see D&C 89:18),
strength in our loins and in our sinews,
(see Job 40:16-17), power in the priesthood,
(see D&C 107:14), nourishment from the
scriptures, and we will be fortified to
endure to the end in righteousness,
to receive the grace of God, and to
enter into His Rest. (See 2
Nephi 31:20).

As we journey through "this vale of tears" (see Wycliffe's Bible, Psalms 84:6), the real journey to Christ has only just begun. Having been born again through baptism, we "press forward" with complete dedication and with "steadfastness," or with confidence, and a firm determination in Christ, "having a perfect brightness of hope," or perfect faith, and charity, or "a love of God and of all men." When we do this, "feasting upon the word of Christ," by receiving nourishment and strength from the scriptures, and if we then endure to the end in righteousness, we "shall have eternal life," which is the greatest of all the gifts that our Heavenly Father can bestow. (2 Nephi 31:20).

By his own agonizingly painful personal experience, Alma understood the principles that are intertwined with real conversion, (see Alma Chapter 36), undergoing a metamorphosis with which many of us can relate. It points us in the direction of humility. We have a conscious and unmistakable recognition of our iniquities, and a deep godly sorrow for our sins. Next comes inescapable suffering that stimulates an appeal to the Savior, together with an awakening understanding of the power of the Atonement. Only then, comes forgiveness, spiritual enlightenment, and great joy. This encourages us to commit or to recommit ourselves to lifestyles of righteousness.

The Book of Mormon
speaks to our spirits, for every gospel
principle carries within itself an independent
witness that it is true. Its language is universal,
and when the Holy Ghost illuminates our minds,
we enjoy fluency, an easy familiarity with the
doctrines, and a comfortable association with
the revealed word of God that opens up
vistas of eternal proportion
before our eyes.

The worth of the doctrines and principles
that are taught by the prophets in The Book of
Mormon is validated through our personal experience
and our subsequent witness. Our desire to embrace them
becomes the outward expression of dedication to obedience.
Ordinances become the public manifestation of our desire
to have a private covenant relationship with God. They
represent the voluntary surrender of our agency to a
higher power, and the subjugation of our will to
His. Our testimonies reflect the promises
and covenants that we make
and keep with God.

In the ultimate
sense, birth is not really a question
of development or of maturation, but rather of
generation. In a long list of emotional, miraculous,
and awe-inspiring experiences, becoming new creatures
in Christ (see Mosiah 27:26) becomes the quintessential
event of mortality. Just so, the process of kindling our
divine spark, of igniting the spirit lying dormant
within us, of awakening our divine potential,
and of nurturing the God in embryo
that is present within each of us,
is described as being
"born again."

The Book of Mormon is of such power
that it drives the law into our inward parts,
so that it is written upon our hearts. A mighty
change takes place as we experience the process of
sanctification. When we've been born again, the
desired result of gospel-oriented teaching has
been achieved, and we'll have no more
disposition to do evil, but to do
good continually. (See
Mosiah 5:2).

The Book of Mormon
replenishes the power cells that fuel
our actions, giving our sight infinite
perspective in the flow of a pulsing stream
of inspiration that has no temporal or spatial
boundary. As we are swept up by quickening
currents into the direct experience of a holy
communion with God, the heady appeal
of the enticements of Satan fades in
the brilliant light of day.

When the laws that relate to the ordinances
of salvation, sanctification, justification, and
exaltation, that are alluded to by the prophets in The
Book of Mormon, have been woven into the sinews of
our souls, that they become essential elements of the
tapestry of our lives and become central to the very
pattern upon which we trace our progress along
the path of progression, our "minds become
single to God, and the days will come
that (we) shall see him, for he will
unveil his face unto (us)."
(D&C 88:68).

Those of us who not only
have eyes to see but also ears
to hear regard The Book of Mormon
like a breath of fresh air. It throws wide
open the windows of understanding, that
we might better comprehend the principles of
the gospel that must forever remain as mysteries
to those who have not spiritually prepared themselves
for personal revelation from God. The Lord has assured
us that we "shall know of a surety that these things are
true, for from heaven will (He) declare it unto (us)."
(D&C 5:12). When we seek to understand, and we
ask as Antionah did of Alma: "What does the
scripture mean?" because of our baptism,
we will comprehend its principles
that relate to doctrine.
(Alma 12:21).

An initial
reading of the Book
of Mormon emancipates us
from self-limiting conditions
that had beforehand blinded us to
a more expansive view of life. It frees
us to pay closer attention to celestial
guideposts and principles. It invites
us to experience more intense and
reflective self-awareness, deeper
and more abiding humility,
reinvigorated confidence,
and incomprehensively
more profound and
enduring faith.

The practical model of
life that is provided by a correct
understanding of the principles and
doctrine that forms the substance of The
Book of Mormon allows us to reconcile our
place in the cosmos with eternity, by giving
us down to earth instruction relating to our
heavenly potential. It gives us the tools to
work out our salvation before the Lord,
even as we deal with the distress of
telestial trivia and grapple with
the distractions of temporal
trauma.

The Book of Mormon
forges a link between the realities
of our physical world and the promises
of eternity, and seamlessly harmonizes
one with the other. It also provides us with
the practical tools we need to hash out the
details of our progression toward that
"undiscovered country from whose
bourn no traveler returns."
(Shakespeare).

Book of Mormon prophets describe what happens when we turn our faces to heaven. Although they will always be higher than ours, God's thoughts will have somehow become our thoughts, and His ways our ways. (See Isaiah 55:8-9). We will be mesmerized by His work and His glory, and will be nudged ever closer to the mind-bending realization that "the universe is a machine for the making of gods." (Henri Bergson).

The principle of opposition that is repeatedly illustrated in Book of Mormon stories clearly points to the Atonement as the only reasonable alternative to an otherwise overwhelmingly negative influence competing for dominance in our lives. It stipulates that we go thru a process of Repentance wherein we Recognize our transgression, experience Remorse, Renounce the self-defeating behavior, Resolve to do better, make Restitution where possible, and then do our part to establish a Reconciliation with the Spirit, ultimately Receiving a Remission of sin through the grace of God our Redeemer.

If the stellar example of the Sons of Mosiah (see Alma 17:2-3) has taught us anything, it is that we must not allow our prejudices to influence the depth of our compassion, or allow debate to determine the merits of the petitions of the impoverished before we decide whether it is prudent to provide them with aid. Ammon, Aaron, Omner, and Himni rightly ignored the protestations of their brethren in Zarahemla who had characterized the wicked Lamanites to whom they desired to minister as "a stiffnecked people, whose hearts delight in the shedding of blood, whose days have been spent in the grossest iniquity, whose ways have been the ways of a transgressor from the beginning." (Alma 26:23-25).

Without the influence of the Savior, to Whom we are introduced in The Book of Mormon, "we wait for light, but behold obscurity; for brightness, but we walk in darkness. We grope for the wall like the blind … as if we had no eyes. We stumble at noonday as in the night. We are in desolate places as dead men. We roar like bears, and mourn sore like doves. We look for judgment, but there is none; for salvation, but it is far off from us. For our transgressions are multiplied before (God), and our sins testify against us." (Isaiah 59:9-12).

The Book of Mormon makes
a resounding statement that when
we have been born of God, it is because we
have received His image in our countenances,
and even more, that we have experienced a mighty
change in our hearts. (See Alma 5:14 & 26). Only
then, through saving faith, will we be prepared to
appropriately exercise our agency to decisively
deal with the opposition that is integral
to the successful execution of the
Plan of Salvation.

The ethereal light that streams
forth from pages of The Book of Mormon
to illuminate the work of God's hands shows us
the way we must go in order to dwell within the secure
fold of the Good shepherd. He is "a lamp unto (our) feet,
and a light unto (our) path." (Psalms 119:105). In the
same vein, we discover that "all things bright and
beautiful, all creatures great and small. All
things wise and wonderful. The Lord
God made them all." (Cecil
Francis Alexander).

The doctrine in The Book of Mormon is the gold
standard for those who have previously identified with
the Pharisees or with the Sadducees, with Buddha, Confucius,
Guru Nanak, Zoroaster, or with gods of wood and stone. It also
supplants the monotheism of Islam and the Bahá'i, the pantheistic
theology of Hinduism, Shintoism, and Taoism, and Eastern
Orthodoxy, as well as secular humanism and irreligion. It
trumps evangelical Christianity, fundamentalism,
Protestantism and Catholicism, as well as
the existential nihilism of the
postmodern world.

Comforter is an appropriate name for the Holy Spirit
or the Holy Ghost, (see Moroni 8:26), for He is the author
of acumen, the avatar of agency, the architect of aptitude, the
benefactor of blessings, the champion of committed Christians,
the craftsman of comfort, the designer of our discipleship, the
engineer of erudition, the guarantor of gifts, the initiator
of insight, the inventor of intelligence, the patron of
perception, the provider of praise, the sponsor of
scholarship, and the ultimate source
of our understanding.

We have observed
repeatedly in The Book
of Mormon how the Devil, when
given the opportunity, capitalizes
on our weaknesses, and uses subtlety,
by pacifying and lulling us into a false
sense of carnal security, making us believe
that we are gaining something when we are
actually losing. He does this to quietly avoid
awakening our faculties to harsh realities.
He distorts our perspective and twists our
very blessings into vehicles that amplify
our feelings of self-sufficiency. Such
emancipation from God comes at the
cost of an ironclad compact that
is made with the author
of sin.

Book of Mormon prophets have
repeatedly invited us to be baptized for "the
remission of sins, (which) bringeth meekness,
and lowliness of heart, and because of meekness
and lowliness of heart cometh the visitation of
the Holy Ghost, which Comforter filleth with
hope and perfect love, which love endureth
by diligence unto prayer, until the end
shall come, when all the saints
shall dwell with God."
(Moroni 8:26).

A dawn of recognition comes
when we study The Book of Mormon,
and in particular when we realize that we
are the "elect according to the foreknowledge
of God the Father, through sanctification of
the Spirit, unto obedience and sprinkling
of the blood of Jesus Christ." (1 Peter 1:2).
We obtain "precious faith," and become
partakers "of the divine nature."
(2 Peter 1:1 & 4).

The sometimes violent confrontation that
occurs between the principles and doctrines that
are taught in The Book of Mormon and the values of
society will tear at the fabric of our world. Our exertion
to remain true to God will test the limits of our stability.
But in the process, we'll find new spiritual strength. When
we go the second mile by lengthening our stride, we burst
free of the shackles that had limited the expression of
our potential. We receive the "gift of spiritual
independence that removes the veil of
insensitivity to our destiny."
(Richard L. Gunn).

The Book of Mormon grounds
us as we struggle to live in the world,
while not falling into the snare of being of the
world. "The worst fear that I have about this people
is that they will get rich in this country, forget God
and his people, wax fat, and kick themselves out of the
church and go to hell. This people will stand mobbing,
robbing, poverty, and all manner of persecution,
and be true. But my greater fear for them is
that they cannot stand wealth."
(Brigham Young).

It was decreed
in heaven before the earth fell
into space that every one of God's
children would have exactly the same
number of hours in each week - 168 to be
exact, and much of it is discretionary time to
do with as they pleased. Every minute is sacred,
but as few as two of these hours are spent in church,
and not many more are typically devoted to scripture
study. We need to ask ourselves: How many hours are
wasted as we 'hang out', or are squandered watching
television, playing video games, or surfing the
net on our computers, or on our mobile
devices, or on social media?

During the creation of the world, God commanded "the greater light to rule the day, and the lesser light to rule the night." (Genesis 1:16). It is illuminating to think of that greater light as the Holy Ghost, and the lesser light as the Light of Christ. The purpose of the lesser light is to lead Heavenly Father's children to His doorstep, where the greater light of the Holy Ghost waits to invite them to enjoy His grace through a portal that the faithful identify as the teachings of The Book of Mormon.

The responsibility of the Holy Ghost is to bear a sacred testimony of the validity of every gospel ordinance. Because there can be no greater witness than that of the Spirit, the Atonement is activated in our behalf by the baptism of fire and of the Holy Ghost. With that unimpeachable witness, Mercy satisfies Justice, and the penitent faithful receive a remission of their sins in a symbolic rite of purification. (See 2 Nephi 31:17).

The Apostle Peter observed: "Of a truth, I perceive that God is no respecter of persons. But in every nation, he that feareth him, and worketh righteousness, is accepted with him." (Acts 10:34-35). When we receive The Book of Mormon as holy scripture, we are converted by the power of the Holy Ghost, and we are carried along on the path leading to eternal life.

In a beautiful admonition to the people of Gideon, Alma described the qualities that we must strive to emulate when we enter the waters of baptism. "Be humble," he pleaded, "and be submissive and gentle; easy to be entreated; full of patience and long-suffering; being temperate in all things; being diligent in keeping the commandments of God at all times; asking for whatsoever things ye stand in need, both spiritual and temporal, always returning thanks unto God for whatsoever things ye do receive. And see that ye have faith, hope, and charity, and then will ye always abound in good works." (Alma 7:23-24).

The sacred mission of
the Holy Ghost is to penetrate
the hard shell of our rough exteriors to
work on what He finds inside of us, namely
our conscience, that He might then gently guide
us beyond the first principles and ordinances of the
gospel, onward and upward to covenants relating to the
priesthood and the temple. "For behold, thus saith the Lord
God: I will give unto the children of men line upon line,
precept upon precept, here a little and there a little, and
blessed are those who hearken unto my precepts,
and lend an ear unto my counsel, for they
shall learn wisdom, for unto him that
receiveth I will give more."
(2 Nephi 28:30).

It is the Light of
Christ that has been benevolently
and universally bestowed upon all of us by
One Whom we can be sure "denieth none that come
unto him, black and white, bond and free, male and
female; and he remembereth the heathen; and all are
alike unto (Him), both Jew and Gentile." (2 Nephi
26:33). It stimulates soul-sweat as it works
on our conscience, our sense of duty, and
our scruples in the face of relentless
opposition in all things.
(See 2 Nephi 2:11).

It is in
The Book of Mormon
where we learn how to "caress
the tender chords of associations, of
gratitude, loyalty, and appreciation, of
selflessness, helpfulness and forgiveness, of
friendship, love, and compassion." It moves us,
with "truth discovered and accepted, of beauty
created and enjoyed, of goodness deepened
and made manifest in life."
(P.A. Anderson).

The Book of Mormon
encourages every one of us to move
beyond our religious roundabouts, to steer
clear of our conceptual cul-de-sacs, and to avoid
the pitfalls of doctrinal dead-ends, that we might
"come unto Christ, (and be) perfected in him, (to)
deny (ourselves) of all ungodliness; and if (we)
shall deny (our)selves of all ungodliness, and
love God with all (our) might, mind and
strength, then is his grace sufficient
for (us), that by his grace (we)
may be perfect in Christ."
(Moroni 10:32).

As we initiate a vigorous dialogue
with those who are struggling to feel even
the influence of the Light of Christ as they make
initial forays into The Book of Mormon, we must not
pretend to know everything. We need to recognize if
we are "speed listening," or formulating retorts in
our mind, when we should instead be listening
carefully. We need to resist the temptation
to treat every conversation as a debate.
As Isaiah counseled: "Come now,
and let us reason together."
(Isaiah 1:18).

The Book of Mormon blesses us with
the capacity to squarely face even our most
stubborn challenges. It helps to be unified with the
Saints, even as we celebrate our individuality and
diversity. It nurtures us to move from dependence,
through independence, and finally to the mature
state of interdependence. It gives us the tools to
enjoy conformity without at the same
time sacrificing what makes
each of us unique.

The truth be told, many of
our friends are very close to receiving
a witness of the truthfulness and divine
origin of The Book of Mormon. If they would
just change one or two behaviors or beliefs, they
would be spot-on. But here's a radical thought,
though. What if, instead, we changed just one
or two of our own behaviors, or we viewed our
neighbors' beliefs in a more tolerant and
ecumenical light? Might that not
become a more powerful tool
of conversion?

The Book of Mormon gives our
spiritual muscles pliancy and flexibility,
that there might be room for the companionship
of the Holy Ghost, "which maketh manifest unto the
children of men, according to their faith." (Jarom 1:4).
We will always be subjected to the effects of adversity
and opposition, but without the therapeutic benefits
of Book of Mormon teachings, we may needlessly
suffer from a stiff neck that prevents us from
looking up to Heavenly Father for guidance,
over to priesthood leaders for counsel,
around to seek out those in need,
and down in an attitude
of humility.

The Last
Days mirror those of
Mormon, who wrote that
"the power of the evil one was
wrought upon all the face of the
land" because of the lack of faith of
the people. (Mormon 1:19). The world
desperately needs The Book of Mormon
because, whether it is aware of it or not,
it is the spiritual equivalent of the boost
that we receive after consuming a power
bar or energy drink 30 minutes before
engaging in physical activity, or
in combat with the Devil.

The Book of Mormon
warns us against succumbing
to a politically correct tolerance that
embraces all sorts of deviant behavior.
There are flim-flam artists abroad in the
land who seek to adroitly fleece us of our very
identity as the children of God, and most of the
time, we are not even aware that the theft is taking
place. "Vice is a monster of such frightful mien, as to
be hated needs but to be seen. Yet seen too oft, familiar
with her face, we first endure, then pity, then embrace."
(Alexander Pope). We have come full circle from Eve's
temptation in the Garden of Eden. Once again, we
are beguiled by the alure of tinkling cymbals
and sounding brass.

The Book
of Mormon will
test the mettle of
our sincerity and our
candor with ourselves. It
is only with our acceptance
of its doctrine, that we place
our money on the Savior. But
we have no proof, or a return on
our investment, until we act on
the basis of trust. Then, comes
the confirmation of the reality
as feelings of self-confidence
grow and purposeful actions
replace tentative overtures.
We are all in; we let go
and let God.

The Book of Mormon teaches that our
little ones are the nobility of heaven, and
members of a chosen generation with divine
destinies. We will make whatever sacrifices are
necessary to ensure their success. They come to
us from their heavenly home "like gentle rain
thru darkened skies, with glory trailing from
their feet as they go, and endless promise in
their eyes." While under our care, they grow
tall and strong, "like silver trees against
the storm; who will not bend with the
wind or the change, but stand
to fight the world alone."
(Doug Stewart).

The age of accountability
to which The Book of Mormon alludes (see
Moroni Chapter 8) suggests that those who are eight
years old are so recently removed from the certainty
and stability of the eternal world, that they are often
impatient to recapture the peaceful security and quiet
serenity of the more relaxed, familiar, and predictable
environment to which they had become accustomed.
Baptism gives them the opportunity to literally
have the best of both worlds; to live on earth,
but still enjoy a heavenly peace that
surpasses understanding.

Not until we have humbly
acknowledged the power of our Father
in Heaven by casting off the self-limiting
conditions and the self-defeating behaviors that
blind us to a larger view of life, will we ever enjoy a
settled conviction of the truth in our minds. The peace
that follows our obedience to the celestial principles that
are illuminated in The Book of Mormon brings a greater
reality within our reach. When we realize that we are not
alone, we have begun a journey that will carry us
to a higher state of being where we will find
ourselves covered in star dust, as we
mingle with the Gods.

It is very likely not lost on
God, Who is, after all, the Creator of both
heaven and earth and all that is therein, (see Mosiah
3:8) that water may just be the most abundant compound
that is found throughout the universe. It should not be lost on
us that baptism by immersion in water for the remission of sins
is His universally recognized token of obedience to gospel principles,
worlds without end. There is no way to know, but it is probably the case
throughout the cosmos. As those who wrote the Serek Scroll described it,
the penitent are "for all the laws of God, and their flesh is cleansed,
shining bright in the waters of purification, even in the waters
of baptism. They shall be given a new name in due time to
walk perfect in all His ways." ("The Serek Scroll," or
"Manual of Discipline," was discovered in 1947,
in caves high above Qumran. It dates
from Book of Mormon times,
around 400 B.C.).

Book of Mormon prophets invite us to
yield ourselves to the promptings of the Holy
Ghost, that we might feel the gentle caress of the
touch of the Master Potter. We find our lives turning
with the hand of time. As the Artisan of our destiny,
our Heavenly Father begins to mold us and shape us.
(See Jeremiah 18:6). We become the clay, and He is
our potter. We are the work of His hands. (See
Isaiah 64:8). As our thoughts turn to Him,
we remain impressionable, and we are
pliable as to the things that relate
to the Spirit.

When we give of ourselves, we create
an independence that can be exhilarating,
because it is accompanied by the recognition of
new-found and soul-expanding opportunities. It
crystalizes within us the realization that we are
spiritual beings having mortal experiences,
ennobling us with the sure knowledge
that only the powers of heaven can
countermand the dizzying
inequities of life.

When a poor, wayfaring man of
grief is down and out, an ounce of help
is always better than a pound of preaching.
As Socrates said: "Know thyself." Cicero urged:
"Control Thyself." But the gospel teaches that we must
give of ourselves. We commemorate our commitment
to actively embrace every demand of discipleship by
following the example of the Savior. After all, "are
we not all beggars? Do we not all depend upon
the same Being, even God, for all the
substance which we have?"
(Mosiah 4:19).

Reflection is a very good
thing when it is the light of Christ that
is brightly shining on our countenances. As
Alma asked the people of Zarahemla, "And now,
behold, I ask of you, my brethren of the church,
have ye spiritually been born of God? Have ye
received His image in your countenances?
Have ye experienced this mighty
change in your heart?"
(Alma 5:14).

With Enos, we "rejoice in
the day when (our) mortal shall
put on immortality, and (we) shall
stand before him; then shall (we) see his
face with pleasure, and he will say unto
(us): Come unto me, ye blessed, there
is a place prepared for you in the
mansions of my Father."
(Enos 1:27).

"For this end was the (Book of Mormon) given," to prepare us to be like the Savior, until "we are made alive in Christ because of our faith." (2 Nephi 25:25).

We mustn't postpone the invitation to secure our testimony of The Book of Mormon until we have become spiritually dead to the Light of Christ. When we no longer are able to make the vital distinction between light and darkness, we risk becoming subject to the wiles of the one who rules the night. (See Alma 34:35).

The Spirit of the Lord
withdraws and Satan has power
over the children of men when they
willfully disparage The Book of Mormon
and lead the children of God astray. This is
the state of the unrepentant wicked, from which
there may be no recovery. When the sword of
Justice falls, for them it will be as if there
had been no redemption made, and the
Atonement will be of no effect.
(See Alma 34:35).

The messages that are woven in to the
monumental themes of The Book of Mormon
are intended to change not only our behavior, but
also our nature. Perfect obedience to its principles and
doctrines qualifies us to enter into the Rest of the Lord.
The covenants that are described therein have power
to move us along the path of progression to the
point that we will internalize God's divine
nature and feel comfortable in His
holy presence.

Book of
Mormon prophets
have inquired of us
if we'll be chaste in our
behavior and if we will love
others; if we will discipline our
nature, and be righteous stewards.
They beg us to love our less fortunate
brothers and sisters, to take proper care
of our bodies, and to try to stay in touch
with the Spirit, to better comprehend God's
omniscience. They invite us to pray for an
understanding of the gift of His Son, and
to ponder the power of His priesthood by
participating in the ordinances
of the gospel.

As we investigate
the themes that trace their way
throughout The Book of Mormon, we
begin to understand how our covenants
with God help us to overcome adversity and
gain self-mastery. We learn that covenants
can help us to focus our efforts to become as
He is. As we do so, it begins to dawn on us
that this is the purpose of the covenants
that we are invited to make with Him.
With a quickening pulse, we begin to
understand that it is our covenants
that prepare us to become as God
is, and to feel comfortable
in His presence.

It seems that whenever the Nephites trivialized celestial sureties, they became more susceptible to the enticements of the Devil. Without the protective influence and guidance of the Holy Ghost, they were vulnerable to the lethal storms sweeping across the face of the earth, which had been initiated by the destroyer. Then, as they lost the power to resist telestial tempests, the suffocating storms of Satan sucked the very life-sustaining marrow from their bones.

Following the post-mortal ministry of the Savior among the Nephites in the land that was round about Bountiful, the powers of heaven and earth amplified each other, and carried them along on the harmonic waves of the Spirit. All their trappings and pretenses were shorn away, outward observances and phylacteries were stripped from the ritual of their worship, and only their true feelings remained.

At a place that was called Mormon, (see Mosiah 18:4), raw and ugly sores that had been inflicted by worldly influences in the court of King Noah were healed in the waters of baptism. The Balm of Gilead prevailed over even the most powerful pestilence that Babylon could muster.

Simply put, The Book of Mormon exposes us to the process by which we progress. Heavenly Father has provided this book in the Last Days to test our mettle. This is why having the courage to be true to our convictions is so intimately tied to gaining a testimony of that book of holy scripture. Only when we act on the basis of faith will we receive a spiritual confirmation of the power that has driven the Restoration forward, as feelings of self-confidence swell within us and our purposeful actions replace our tentative overtures.

The relevancy of King Benjamin's counsel to the people in the land of Zarahemla is self-evident: "This much I can tell you," he said. "If ye do not watch yourselves, and your thoughts, and your words, and your deeds, and observe the commandments of God, and continue in the faith … even unto the end of your lives, ye must perish." (Mosiah 4:30).

There is a veritable groundswell of emotion that is stimulated by the Light of Christ. It generates the energy to carry us heavenward in the direction of a testimony of The Book of Mormon. Our worship is elevated to something more dynamic than the simple mechanical observance of a multiplicity of ceremonial rules. Seeking the guidance of the Holy Ghost as we study is the daily antidote to our tendency toward pride, selfishness, and self-reliance.

One of the problems that was faced by the Nephites was that they often failed to generate the spiritual horsepower to express their feelings about the Savior. Such was the case when Jesus asked the Pharisees: "What think ye of Christ? Whose son is he?" (Matthew 22:41-42). Sadly, their sluggish response was tendered with little feeling or emotion. Its dearth of traction was obvious, its inability to generate spontaneity was palpable, its lack of energy to engage enthusiasm was noticeable, its incapacity to spark vitality was evident, and its failure to candidly acknowledge the powerful relationship that could have existed between themselves and God was clear.

The innocuous question posed by the Savior: "What think ye of Christ?" (see Matthew 22:42 & Alma 5:20) has always demanded of Pharisees, Nephites, and others that they dig deeply within themselves as they have been invited to bear their witness, because it is all too easy to stammeringly retreat into colorless and insipid verbiage as the easy way out. No matter who we might be, if we casually and carelessly steer a course away from Him with offhand, dismissive, or inconsiderate comments, until He is conveniently out of sight and mind, we can realistically expect in return no more than a stupor of thought.

When we enthusiastically
embrace The Book of Mormon,
we unleash a spiritual cornucopia.
We feast upon the nourishing bread of
life that has been provided, drink from a
well of living water, and with renewed
energy, we "lift up (our) heads and
receive the pleasing word of God,
and feast upon His love."
(Jacob 3:2).

Those who have accepted the challenge of
the missionaries to read The Book of Mormon with
an open mind and heart stand out in contrast to those
undisciplined souls who have been seduced by the siren song
of Satan's sentinels. Without the stabilizing influence of the
gospel, unprincipled character crumbles when faced with telestial
temptations that are tantalizing and yet traumatizing. These
treasures of the earth are worthless counterfeits for the
blessings that God has reserved for the faithful.
It is this substitution of the sacred by the
profane that is an abomination
in the sight of God.

The Nephites' observance
of the Law of the Sabbath introduced
them to a day of worship and of rest, that
they might find refuge far from the tumult of
the teeming multitudes of the maddingly telestial
crowd. Their observance protected them from choking
on possessions whose opacity might have otherwise
clouded their ability to experience illumination
by the Spirit. Focusing on the kingdom, and
especially on the Sabbath, helped them to
maintain their perspective and to
strengthen their reverence
for the work.

Too often, it seems that the Nephites
quite painfully recognized that they had
sought "all the days of (their) lives for that
which (they could not) obtain, and … ha(d)
sought for happiness in doing iniquity,
which thing is contrary to the nature
of that righteousness which is in
our great and Eternal Head."
(Helaman 13:38).

The Book of Mormon provides valuable insight into the spiritual roots of our relationships that are the products of interconnectivity and interdependence. These are essential if we want to live in the world without being tarnished by it. In the end, abundance will be "multiplied unto (all those who have taken the time and make the effort to study the scriptures) through the manifestations of the Spirit." (D&C 70:13). Righteous objectives stay in focus when we pay attention to the guideposts that have been so abundantly provided in the book. These mile markers help us to stay on track during our journey through mortality.

In The Book of Mormon, we find illustrations of Nephites who lived "after the manner of happiness" for a season. (2 Nephi 5:27, also see 3 Nephi 27:11, Alma 41:11, & Helaman 13:38). This was possible only because their levels of understanding and their behavior harmonized with worldly parameters. As long as they could shut out the light of Christ, they lived the illusion of happiness. But, ultimately, the discrepancy between their errant behavior and foundation gospel principles became so great that their deviant lifestyles couldn't be sustained, because their short-lived pleasure in worldly ways was strangled by sin. As they came up fighting for air, many of them gaspingly realized that "wickedness never was happiness." (Alma 41:10).

The Book of Mormon is a divine portal to the principles, ordinances, and covenants that enable us to be sanctified, to one day be worthy to live once again in a state of holiness in the presence of our Heavenly Father. By following its teachings, all may come unto Christ, and lay hold upon every good gift ... and be perfected in him, (as they) deny (themselves) all ungodliness." (Moroni 10:30 & 32). Because of that book, we may all "continue in the supplicating of his grace" to one day stand blameless before Him at His Pleasing Bar. (See Alma 7:3).

When we stand in holy places, and we are freed from the cares and concerns of the world, the realities of eternity will illuminate our minds. As we read The Book of Mormon, if we listen very carefully, we can hear the gentle rustling of the wings of angels coming from behind a slightly-parted veil. The company of beings from the unseen world sweeps the cobwebs from our minds that opens up to our view undreamed vistas of otherwise inaccessible experience.

As we read The Book of Mormon, we are invited to consider the possibility that we might in a coming day be like our Savior Jesus Christ, that is, holy and without spot, because of His Atonement. We believe that His grace consists of the gifts and power by which we may be brought to His perfection and stature, so that we may enjoy not only what He has, but also what He is. We believe in His promise: "If ye by the grace of God are perfect in Christ, and deny not his power, then are ye sanctified in Christ by the grace of God, through the shedding of the blood of Christ, which is in the covenant of the Father unto the remission of your sins, that ye become holy, without spot."
(Moroni 10:33).

Those who undertake a serious study of The Book of Mormon will very quickly see that it is not prejudicial. It doesn't play favorites nor does it pick sides. It simply levels the playing field for all of Heavenly Father's children. He knows that His Merciful Plan has enough wiggle room to allow our agency to find expression in myriad ways. The principles and doctrines found within its pages will always stand ready to guide us to a testimony of Jesus Christ, but in the meantime, we remain free to worship Almighty God according to the dictates of our own conscience. The "Author of Eternal Salvation" allows us to worship how, where, or what we may. (Hebrews 5:9, see also the 11th Article of Faith).

It is our hope in Jesus Christ
(see Moroni 7:3) that is buttressed by
the foundation scriptures in The Book of
Mormon. Our desire to believe is not wishful
thinking, nor is it misguided trust in promises
that cannot be fulfilled, and it is not a high-stakes
gamble that is based on statistical improbabilities.
It is the inevitable reward of well-founded faith, when
we have developed the discipline to completely control
the innate thrust within us, and to channel it in
the direction of testimony, and to keep our
priorities and desires in harmony
with gospel principles.

If we let it to work its magic to change
our hearts, The Book of Mormon can become a
catalyst that propels us upward toward the discovery
of personal levels of experience with the Savior, for when
scriptures speak of "knowing Him," they must be referring
to a very special sense of the word. It is not enough that we
know about Him by reading the Gospels, or by listening
to others speak of Him. We must know Him through the
bonds of common experience and common feeling.
Thus, our familiarity with the book, which is a
Second Witness of Jesus Christ, becomes
an immersion in the tangible
element of Spirit.

The Book of Mormon is far more
involved with recovery than it is with discovery. Its
objective is not union, but reunion with divine realities.
The religious recognition that we experience when reading the
book is a re-learning of that which we have already understood.
It is in this context that the word 'religion' may derive from the
Latin root "ligare" - "to bind." Thus religion would mean
"to bind again." This fits nicely with the perspective
that links religion to a reunion with a divine
purpose, or a Plan, for Heavenly
Father's children.

The prophets of The Book of Mormon
invite us over and over again to do more than
make resolutions that are too often nothing more
than empty promises to ourselves that are generally
kept for only a few days or weeks at best, before they are
abandoned and we return to our previously held lifestyles.
The book's emphatic presentation of principles and doctrine
has real staying power. It has no bias; its basis is belief,
nurtured by a rich culture medium that has been
infused with the agar of faith, repentance
and the companionship of the Spirit.
(See the 4th Article of Faith).

For many sincere souls who
are inquiring after truth, following
their introduction to The Book of Mormon,
the feelings they would like to express cannot be
formed into words. Suffice to say, that by the grace
of God, their eyes have been opened. The Savior becomes
their traveling companion and trusted Advisor. He helps
them to forget their bad days and to become better; to
love their families, and to be more responsible
towards others. In a word, to sacrifice
themselves through the love
of the Lord.

In the months following the
publication of The Book of Mormon,
gone were the days when those who had been
earnestly seeking the truth could remain content
to build upon the sepulchres of the fathers. No longer
would they be satisfied by reading histories, biographies,
and criticisms relating to the mission of the Savior and His
gospel. Third-person accounts would no longer suffice. All of
a sudden, The Book of Mormon stood as a testament that it
was now possible to individually and institutionally
tap directly into fountains of living water.

The Greatest
Story Ever Told
is an appellation that
has been ascribed, not only
to the Bible, but also to The Book
of Mormon. Both scriptures are meant
to be signs and wonders to an unbelieving
world. The Book of Mormon, in particular, was
given to give guidance to true believers in the Last
Days. It is a story for good times and for hard times.
It has the power to dismiss worldly influences that
compete with its issues of real substance, for
example, that the heavens are once again
open, and should become the focus
of our attention.

With the Book of Mormon, each of us has been
fitted with a shield of faith that has been tailored to our
unique needs. Its elements are strengthened by covenants
that we make with Heavenly Father that form the foundation
of the book. We make these individually, and not collectively,
and we review and renew them repetitively. This protects us from
getting caught up in the mechanics of the church, from killing
the articles of its faith, and from permitting form to triumph
over spirit. The kingdom is built by something as simple as
our ardor and conviction, as we consciously nurture our
relationship with God in a process that informally
begins with a testimony of The Book of
Mormon, and formally begins
with our baptism.

By its very nature, the existence of The Book of Mormon has contributed to "a great division among the people." (2 Nephi 30:10). In the Last Days, its adversaries are jockeying for position to control our minds, just as they did during our pre-mortal lives. Combatants with increasingly polarized ideologies are forming ranks, in preparation for a battle that has already commenced. (See Revelation 16:14).

Those who have read and prayed about The Book of Mormon will often testify that it has compelled them to internalize gospel principles. It teaches them to view their lives from an eternal perspective, which makes it easier to discern the polarized opposites that are so prevalent in our society today. When we see through the clarifying lens of faith, we can more easily distinguish happiness from its worldly counterfeits, such as pleasure, desire, decadence, sensuality, gratification, indulgence, carnality, and amusement. The Book of Mormon makes it possible, when we are weighed in the balances after living in the world, to be spiritually quickened.

When we sit down to seriously read and
study The Book of Mormon, our religious recognition
will be mystically transformed into a re-cognition and
a re-knowing, and its principles and doctrine will become the
sum and substance of our existence. The Holy Ghost will help us
to deal with our natural inclination to suppress that instinctive
response. If, in any way, we make an attempt to thwart the
intrinsic Light of Christ, we will be "accountable, and
to a degree, we will condemn ourselves. We knew
Christ before this life, we know Him here, and
we will know Him hereafter. His sheep
do indeed know His voice."
(Truman Madsen).

Every now and then, we will
confront a Doubting Thomas who
demands physical proof relating to
The Book of Mormon as a condition for
their belief. They seek to circumvent the
process by which faith and knowledge
are developed. They demand proof but
refuse to pay the price. As with the
adulterer, they seek the result
without accepting the
responsibility.

It was never intended that a testimony
of The Book of Mormon should follow the receipt
of signs from heaven. Instead, our faith precedes the
miracle. Spiritual confirmation always flows along the
pathway that has been created by faith. If a witness were
given before faith had transformed us, we might have
sure knowledge. But it would have come without an
expenditure of faith, and so there would be no
appreciation of its significance. It is
faith that infuses our belief
with staying power.

The Book of Mormon
grounds us to practical belief, but
with elements that commit us to a path
that will lead "Citius, Altius, and Fortius."
However, our subsequent works will not assure us
of salvation, nor will they make us good. It is the grace
of God that does so. (See 2 Nephi 25:23). Wresting the
scriptures by suggesting that we are somehow saved
by our works, twists holy writ from its true or its
or proper signification, and perverts it from its
correct application. Notwithstanding our
faith, we are saved by the grace of
God, after all we can do.

Rather than simply multiplying mirrors and manipulating angles without increasing the light, The Book of Mormon facilitates the illumination of our minds by the Spirit. We have no proof until we act on the basis of belief. Then comes the ratification of the reality, that is manifest as a spiritual confirmation, but only after we act in faith. That is the essence of why James taught that "faith, if it hath not works, is dead, being alone." (James 2:17).

Gaining a testimony of The Book of Mormon's divine authenticity is the outward evidence of our exercise of faith. As we lift the latch and we force the way, we gain spiritual maturity until our faith becomes perfect knowledge. Initially, faith is to believe what we do not see, and the reward of our faith is to see what we believe. The process by which faith is developed is one of testing. The Lord gives certain principles, and by obedience to them, blessings and power follow.

The marvel of God's
love is that the more we try
to understand and do His will,
the more He blesses us. Therefore, we
become even more deeply indebted to Him,
and we remain so forever. That debt remains
completely beyond our ability to pay. We can
do nothing that puts Him in our debt. But
God does not ask us to settle our account
with Him. He only asks that we
keep His commandments.

When we initiate what may turn out to
be a lifetime study of The Book of Mormon, we
need to be aware that temporal baggage can create
imbalance that leads to confusion. Our engagement
with the book jars us out of our collective complacency
by upsetting the stagnation of the status quo. With the
guidance of the Spirit, we are invited to enjoy a settled
conviction in our minds as our juices begin to flow.
The Holy Ghost prods us to constructively
expend our energy and put our
agency to work.

The riches of eternity (see Alma 32:42-43) may represent something that is as simple as the blessing to see from the perspective of God. The Book of Mormon helps to bring these treasures within our grasp, by expanding our vision beyond physical laws that pertain only to the temporal world, toward an appreciation of gospel principles that relate to the eternities. It invites us to touch the garment of the Savior, not with one of the mean five physical senses, but with our incorruptible spiritual sixth sense.

God allows us to live in the world as long as our feet are firmly planted on gospel sod and we recognize sounding brass and tinkling cymbals for what they really are. The Book of Mormon can help to catalyze a mystical and metaphysical transformation wherein we may be figuratively born of God, so that, with new eyes, we can more clearly see what is before us. (See Mosiah 5:7).

The Book
of Mormon will
help us to appreciate
that we are here, at this
place, and in this time, by
divine design. What we think
are only coincidences if they are
instead viewed thru the clarifying
lens of eternity, are faith promoting
examples of the Lord patiently working
behind the scenes in our behalf. Nothing
in our lives happens by chance. While we
are not billiard balls, it is equally true
that most, if not all, of the things that
are of significance to us will happen
according to the perfect Plan of
our Heavenly Father.

While it seems to be our lot in life to face
opposition, we are not truly learned, and we
are not really strong, unless we hearken to the
Savior's counsel The principles and doctrine of
The Book of Mormon quicken us, that we might
use opposition as the key it was intended to be,
to open up a portal to the Spirit. We thereby
internalize those principles, we retain
ownership, and in our obedience, we
find the power to do all things.
(See Philippians 4:13).

It is our purposeful study as well as
our engagement with The Book of Mormon that
fuels our actions, charging our spiritual batteries
and energizing our vision with infinite perspective,
creating a pulsing stream of inspiration whose flow
has no temporal or spatial boundary. As we study
and learn, we are engulfed by "the grace of the
Lord Jesus Christ, and the love of God, and
the communion of the Holy Ghost."
(2 Corinthians 13:14).

Heavenly Father has quickened our
minds with the ability to resonate with
recognition when they encounter truth and
concentrate on matters of importance, so that
ultimately "every one that hearkeneth to the voice
of the Spirit (will eventually come) unto God, even
the Father." (D&C 84:47). As we study The Book of
Mormon, we'll "discard the poor lenses of the body,
and peer through the telescope of truth into
the infinite reaches of immortality"
with an eternal perspective.
(Helen Keller).

When we are zealous in
our Book of Mormon study, we
become very susceptible to catching a
religious fever that elevates our testimony
temperature just enough to bless us with a sure
witness of the truth. It is one that will get our juices
flowing with an appreciation of the might, majesty,
and dominion of the Savior. (See Alma 23:6). Only
then, will we experience the earth shaking and mind
bending theophany that leaves us with a witness
that we are His spiritual offspring. Only then,
will we recognize the potential energy
of our position, and be prepared to
act accordingly.

We determine to engage The
Book of Mormon because none of us would
knowingly choose to follow a pathway that left
us spiritually depleted. we would never wish to perish
because of our neglect of the things that mattered most.
We understand the consequences of spiritual starvation,
of doctrinal dehydration, and of intellectual inhibition.
Without the book, we risk living marginalized lives
while only inches away from the bread that would
have satisfied our hunger, and fulfilled our
craving for the words of eternal life, and
from healing fountains of living
water that could have slaked
our spiritual thirst.

As we consider what we have gained
when we have studied The Book of Mormon,
perhaps we will intuitively respond to President
Gordon B. Hinckley's invitation to do a little better,
to be a little more kind, to be a little more merciful,
and a little more forgiving; "to put behind us our
weaknesses of the past, and go forth with new
energy and increased resolution to improve
the world about us, in our homes, in our
places of employment," and "in
our social activities."

The Book of Mormon invites us to step
back, take a moment, inhale deeply, and
focus on what is of importance in our busy
lives. Its guiding principles gently envelop us
within the warm embrace of daily spiritual
experiences that confirm our faith.
(See Mosiah 27:33).

We cannot barter the treasures of
the earth with the money changers in the
temple in the hope of receiving spiritual gifts in
the exchange. Perhaps this is why in their efforts to
obtain the sacred records that had been left behind in
Jerusalem, Lehi's sons were stripped by Laban of all
their gold, silver, and precious things. Obtaining
the Holy Scriptures, and devouring them as
the bread of life, was to be accomplished
in the Lord's way, by the power
of His mighty arm.

The pathway that
stretches out before those who've
undertaken a comprehensive study
of The Book of Mormon is the one that
leads to the Tree of Life. It isn't a freeway,
but a toll road. Until we have paid the price,
we cannot hope to comprehend with fluency
the language of the Spirit that clearly
explains how to make our way to the
tree, that we might harvest
its delicious fruit.

Those
who have created
The Book of Mormon
by amassing the records
of a thousand years of history
can be likened to gifted seamstresses.
(See Ether 15:11). They have coherently
stitched together foundation principles and
doctrine into patterns that are understandable
and unambiguous, so that the power of the
word and its witness of truth may be
conveyed to readers in the last
days without the need for
external warrant.

When immersing
ourselves in the study
of The Book of Mormon, the
clarity of our vision gives us the
ability to overcome our weaknesses.
Stumbling blocks become stepping
stones, and through experience,
we learn that "all things which
are good cometh of Christ."
(Moroni 7:24).

The Book of Mormon is absolutely non-discriminatory as far as its audience is concerned. It was designed to be read by the world's heaviest person, who weighed in at 1,400 pounds, by the world's tallest person, who stood 8 feet 11 inches tall, by the world's wealthiest person, who boasts $230 billion in assets, by the world's smartest person whose I.Q. is 230, as well as by the other 8 billion of us who fall somewhere within these extremes.

Living water is so crucial to our well-being that our Father has provided the means for it to penetrate solid limestone, as it were, so that it might flow freely into our lives. The Book of Mormon is one of His tools that is powerful enough to creates a conduit that He has chiseled through our rough exterior and our stony nature. All that is required to activate in our behalf God's artesian well of gospel doctrine is faith, obedience, study, prayer, and good works.

All of the children of God are entitled
to enjoy the influence of the Light of Christ.
There are no scholastic prerequisites relating to the
Plan of Salvation. Those without formal education
are welcome to participate, as are those with advanced
degrees from the most prestigious institutions of
higher learning. It is the poor in spirit, however,
those with broken hearts and contrite spirits,
who seem to have an advantage when
it comes to acting upon their
immortal longings.

When we lose sight of our
righteous objectives, we lose the power
to bring about positive change. An initial
foray into The Book of Mormon however,
sharpens our perspective, enabling us to
comprehend and build upon principles
of perfection that are validated by
the Spirit and emulated by the
example of the Savior.

Turning our attention to the
weightier matters of the law that
permeate The Book of Mormon gives
us a sense of independence, as we learn
something new every day. Learning how to
use our time to our best advantage can open
our hearts and our minds to a breathtaking
expansion of our understanding. As we
adopt a learning style that embraces
the Spirit, we discover the pattern
of heaven, and it becomes
our norm.

The Book of Mormon
rivets our attention on our Heavenly
Father's great gift of happiness that accompanies
untroubled souls. We use our free will to choose the
Savior and yield our hearts to Him. We ponder the great
and terrible consequences of Gethsemane, and we travel the
Via Dolorosa with Him to Calvary. We enjoy the sweetness of the
redeeming power of His Atonement, which is the keystone of the
Plan. We determine to keep the laws of God, because we
have learned that the gospel transcends temporal
security and worldly comforts. Jacob described
these feelings as "that happiness which
is prepared for the saints."
(2 Nephi 9:43).

We very quickly recognize the pathway before us that leads to spiritual transformation and a Christ-centered life. Internalizing the principles and doctrines of The Book of Mormon makes it easier for us to regularly recommit ourselves to internalize its truths and principles relating to eternal progression, and it endows us with the power to endure to the end in righteousness. Some may consider these burdens to be too heavy, but countless witnesses have testified how obedience can become the perfect law of liberty.
(See James 1:25).

Christ is the Author of Salvation, (Hebrews 5:9), and the Finisher of our Faith, (Hebrews 12:2), but the Plan was introduced to His spirit children by Heavenly Father. (See 2 Nephi 9:13). It is by the spirit of revelation that the Holy Ghost testifies of the Savior and of the Father's Plan. (D&C 8:2-3). Working in perfect harmony, the three members of the Godhead promote the doctrine of Christ with one shared goal: to bring us via the waters of baptism to the portals of the Celestial Kingdom.

We who were in attendance at the
Council, who so readily and enthusiastically
raised our arms to the square to support our Father's
proposal, must have felt the import of the moment, when
our Elder Brother Jesus Christ made history. (See Job
38:7). In fact, He was creating a binding precedent
to re-write history itself. We were eyewitnesses
to the vitalization of "The Merciful Plan of
The Great Creator" that is described
in The Book of Mormon.
(2 Nephi 9:6).

There are no shades of grey after we have
received a testimony of the divine authenticity of
The Book of Mormon, and our hearts and our minds
have become "single to God." (D&C 88:68). If, later,
we try to have it both ways, our double mindedness
will create intellectual instability and spiritual
schizophrenia, for we cannot be servants
of the Devil while purporting
to follow Christ.

Evil people can
do good, but in the end their works
are a blessing neither to themselves nor
to those whom they pretend to serve. When
a good deed is motivated by selfish desire, it
lacks the power to enrich or transform the
giver, and it is "not counted unto
him for righteousness."
(Moroni 7:7).

We particularly need the gift of
discernment when dealing with a media that
has done an excellent job of confusing issues of
importance. We remember the caution of Mormon,
who, with a prescient glimpse into our day, wrote:
"Wherefore, take heed, my beloved brethren, that
ye do not judge that which is evil to be of
God, or that which is good and of
God to be of the Devil."
(Moroni 7:14).

As seekers of truth study The
Book of Mormon, the Light of Christ may be the
sole source of their inspiration. They get by with the
tools they have been given. They take consolation
in the fact that Moroni taught that we "should
search diligently in the light of Christ, that
(we) may know good from evil."
(Moroni 7:18-19).

Those who initiate an investigation
of the merits of The Book of Mormon must
venture forth out of the shadows if they want
to appreciate the special familiarity that the Lord
enjoys with those whom He has characterized as
"the children of light." (John 12:36). As they
describe to others how they feel about Christ,
they learn to recognize the awakening
sensations that come naturally as
a result of the stirrings of deep
feelings of intimacy.

3 Nephi Chapter 8 describes the destruction that occurred in Book of Mormon lands. It appears to have been one of the greatest natural disasters in the history of the world. It was the physical manifestation of the earth's revolt against the crucifixion of its Creator. Perhaps the record of the experience of the Nephites is as close as any of us will come to understanding just how overwhelming will be the spiritual darkness that is going to prevail among those who are resurrected to a kingdom without glory, which is as a "lake which burneth with fire and brimstone, which is the second death." (D&C 63:17).

The thought is developed through repetition, and it builds to a climax with the additional material that's been presented as the verse reaches its conclusion. In other words, the second unit partially balances the first, but also adds a summary thought or completes the series.

Those who have embraced
The Book of Mormon as holy scripture,
and have received the blessings that heaven "has
in store for the faithful, will be able to know the things
of God from the things which are not of God, the light from
the darkness, that which comes from heaven, and that which
comes from somewhere else. This is the satisfaction and the
consolation that the Latter-day Saints enjoy by living
their religion. This is the knowledge which
everyone who thus lives, possesses."
(Brigham Young).

What should we do if we are faced with
opportunities in life that just seem too good
to be true?. Sometimes, the very "deceitfulness
of riches choke(s) the word," and we are blinded to
our characteristic good judgment, insomuch that
we act irrationally. (Matthew 13:22). That is to
say, the temptation of screaming deals can
cloud our vision and compromise our
ability to make correct and
prudent choices.

Speaking to us from eternity, the Savior promised: I will go before your face (and) will be on your right hand, and on your left, and my Spirit shall be in your hearts, and mine angels round about you, to bear you up." (D&C 84:88). With such assurance, how could we imagine to turn away from our Book of Mormon studies, to persist in our wickedness, and to deceive ourselves by believing that we could fly solo, without the safety that is provided by His Atonement's parachute?

God is sensitive to our needs, and does hear our prayers. In conformity to some spiritual law, we can tap into and draw upon the life force that is the Spirit of God. When we do so, we are, in effect, touching His garment.

As we ponder The
Book of Mormon, we
would do well to organize
ourselves, and prepare every
needful thing as we establish a
house of prayer, fasting, faith,
learning, glory, and order; in
other words, as we seek to
establish a house of
God. (See D&C
88:119).

In the
Book of Mormon, we
learn that God in heaven is
the Grand Architect of a divine
design that establishes our familial
roots and confirms His fatherhood, that
we might enjoy a witness that it is in Him
alone that "we live, and move, and have
our being; as certain also of (our) own
poets have said. For we are also his
offspring." (Acts 17:28).

We will
not endure
for long if we
rely only upon the
light that is generated
by our casual connections
to our Father in Heaven. He'll
provide our external power source
with ample energy for as long as we
manifest a desire to become members
of His Second Mile Club, which is a
privileged group to which we have
been invited, in consequence
of our acceptance of The
Book of Mormon.

Our
physical
surroundings in
this lone and dreary
world have been designed,
harsh though they may seem,
to provide a hint of familiarity.
We are sensitive to the Spirit as we
read and study The Book of Mormon,
and we establish a celestial connection
as we commune with the heavens across
space and time, bursting the barriers
of our telestial habitation.

The Book of
Mormon frees us, not
only from the limitations
of our own ignorance, but also
from the constraints of mortality.
It is in the scriptures that we learn to
be at one with the majestic clockwork,
"like a bird that, pausing in her flight
a while on boughs to light, feels them
give way beneath her and yet sings,
knowing that she hath wings."
(Victor Hugo).

In Third Nephi, we
read about those who survived the
chaos in the land after the crucifixion
of the Lord. From the unseen world, "there
was a voice heard among all the inhabitants
of the earth, upon all the face" of the land. (3
Nephi 9:1). It was not the deafening voice of a
hundred decibels, but simply a quiet sound
that was heard by everyone regardless of
their temporal surroundings. It was a
voice quite unlike any sound that
had ever before been heard, for
it came from immortal lips
with an effect on heaven
and earth that was
profound.

When we stand before the
Judgment Bar of God, we will concede that
the covenants to which we had been introduced
within the pages of The Book of Mormon were neither
haphazard nor arbitrary. There were neither corollaries
and footnotes, nor addenda and exceptions to the rule. Our
obedience had demanded neither analytics nor explanation by
legal counsel, and its accounting required no interpretation by
an expensive C.P.A. The ordinances had been clearly established
and carefully clarified with purposeful precision so that there
could be no disputation concerning their accessibility
or validity. In every sense of the word, God is
no respecter of persons, and He dots every
'I' and crosses every 'T'.

It is
in The Book
of Mormon where
we take our bearings
on eternity. We get a fix
on the stars in the heavens.
Within its pages, our telestial
tendencies are transformed into
celestial sureties with the spiritual
equivalents of compasses, protractors,
chronometers, sextants, chart dividers, and
rulers. This process is not one of maturation
but of generation, to the extent that we are
'born again' in a house of learning that
also serves as a delivery room for our
spirits. Thus, we will also need the
spiritual equivalents of forceps,
clamps, catheters, and
specula.

At the end of
our mortal journey, .
we will remember that it
was the counsel of The Book
of Mormon that channeled us
past the doctrinal dead ends, as
well as through the conceptual cul
de sacs and telestial traffic jams, that
always threatened to detour us from the
strait and narrow way. We will be forever
grateful for the holy scriptures that exposed
us to direct experience with the perfect law of
liberty, and that permitted us to exchange
the uncertain course adopted by those
who were bound for the telestial
kingdom, for the reality of
celestial surety.

As we
look about
us, at a world
that seems to have
gone mad, The Book
of Mormon stands as
a light that has been set
on a hill. As an island in a
storm, it provides refuge from
the uncertainties of life and the
vagaries of men. It speaks in a
language of stability, purpose,
and direction to all those who
might be afraid, hesitant,
and uncertain during
a crisis of their
faith.

We see in The Book of Mormon indistinct hints of those who sought to harness the power of the priesthood, "to break mountains, to divide the seas, to dry up waters, to turn them out of their course; to put at defiance the armies of nations, to divide the earth, to break every band, to stand in the presence of God, to do all things according to his will, according to his command, subdue principalities and powers; and this by the will of the Son of God which was from before the foundation of the world. And (those with) this faith, coming up unto this order of God, were translated and taken up into heaven." (J.S.T. Genesis 14:30-32, see Alma Chapter 13).

For many of us, perhaps for most of us, it will only be during our journey to the veil that will have been accompanied by our study of The Book of Mormon, that we will comprehend how we might one day "flourish in immortal youth, unhurt amidst the war of elements, the wreck of matter, and the crash of worlds." (Joseph Addison).

Millions have discovered that
it has largely been within the pages
of The Book of Mormon that their souls
have been liberated to go forth from their
dwelling places. They have discarded
the poor lenses of the body, to peer
thru the telescope of truth into
the expansive reaches of
immortality.

Our
acceptance of
Alma's invitation to
enter into the waters of
baptism is life-sustaining
and life-generating, for just as
we are "born into the world by water,
and of blood, and the spirit" and have
become of dust living souls, even so, we
"must be born again into the kingdom of
heaven, of water, and of the Spirit, and
be cleansed by blood," even the blood of
Jesus our Redeemer, that we "might be
sanctified from all sin, and enjoy
the words of eternal life in this
world, and eternal life in the
world to come." (Moses
6:59-60).

As we engage the Book of Mormon, we embark upon an incredible journey through thousands of years of history, as the pages of a most profound text unfold before the panorama of great civilizations. Within its pages lies the intrigue of ancient Asia as warlords battle for supremacy and tension in Jerusalem rises as empires of the Near East struggle for power. We witness the thrill of those whose eyes were fixed on a Land of Promise beyond the horizon of their vision, and we feel the exhilaration of prophets of God who counseled all mankind. Those who truly appreciate it, will feast upon the word of God and devour the book as if it were literally the bread of life. They will seek, and yearn, and strive, and wrestle for their blessing.

The Book of Mormon makes the bold claim that its pages contain the fulness of the gospel. (See D&C 42:12). Even members of The Church of Jesus Christ of Latter-day Saints sometimes misinterpret this. It does not mean that there will be found on its pages detailed instruction regarding every doctrinal principle, nor does it mean that the Nephites participated in every ordinance of the gospel, as we know it. Today, we live in the Dispensation of the Fulness of Times, when all that has been revealed throughout the ages will be given. The members of the church in Book of Mormon times were given knowledge sufficient for their own salvation. More properly, this is the context within which the definition 'the fulness of the gospel' makes the most sense.

There is unity within the
church regarding the religious dogma
that's embedded within The Book of Mormon.
Every day all over the world, millions of Latter-
day Saints open their translations of this scripture
and explore identical doctrinal themes. Contrast this
unity of the faith with the thousands of denominations
who interpret with significant differences hundreds of
variants of single biblical verses of scripture. It is far
better for the church to proclaim that The Book of
Mormon was translated by the gift and power
of God through the Prophet Joseph Smith.
This leaves little room for doctrinal
interpretation either within or
outside the church.

We left our heavenly home
with assurances from our Father that,
while on earth, we would have the Light of
Christ and the influence of the Holy Ghost,
and that heavenly power would help us
to recognize the truth when we heard
it. As Brigham Young declared:
"Every gospel principle carries
within it a witness that
it is true."

The Book
of Mormon is
like a stethoscope
that has the ability to
measure our cardiac vital
capacity. When our hearts
have broken in contrition,
we're able to detect a steady
sinus rhythm confirming
the congruence that must
exist between ourselves
and the greater light
of heaven.

The Book of Mormon
tenderly lifts us to higher
ground, to our own Mount of
Transfiguration. When we reach
its spiritual plateau, our faces will
shine and our raiment will radiate
with a dazzling glow that could
only have been kindled by one
source, which is the glory of
God's celestial fire.

Because The Book of Mormon is more than just history, and because it is another testament, or second witness, of Jesus Christ, it is used to great effect as a principal tool of conversion. The book was inspired to assist God as He continues to perform His work to bring to pass our immortality and eternal lives, by teaching the principles of faith, repentance, baptism, and the ordinances of the priesthood. There was method to his madness when Mormon abridged the records with which Ammaron had entrusted him.

One thing that is important to our comprehension of the monumental themes addressed in The Book of Mormon is familiarity with the underlying structure of the text. It is not too difficult to understand, as long as we remember that Mormon was the prophet who gathered all the records together, and who then abridged certain of these into the Plates of Mormon. This is the main reason why the text is called The Book of Mormon. In a larger sense, though, it is not really his book alone.

Mormon said that he couldn't write "the hundredth part of the things of (his) people." (Words of Mormon 1:5). Even though Joseph wrote in his history that the plates on the Hill Cumorah were deposited in the earth in a box fashioned out of stone, other sources indicate that there were many more plates at that site. Brigham Young said that there was a whole room, with plates stacked high against the walls. Together, he said that they would comprise several wagon-loads.

What we do have swells in significance with the realization that the fraction of the record that was included in the book is a condensation which comprises only the history that Mormon considered to be of most importance to those living in the last days.

Without The Book of Mormon, our age would continue to be insufferably and mind-numbingly retrospective. It would build only upon the sepulchres of the fathers. Without The Book of Mormon, we would have at our disposal nothing but biographies, histories, and criticisms. The ancients beheld the God of Abraham, Isaac, and Jacob face to face; but we would only see Him through their eyes. "But why should we not also enjoy an original relation to the universe? Why should we not have a poetry and philosophy of insight and not only of tradition, and a religion by revelation to us, and not just the history of theirs?" (Ralph Waldo Emerson). Such is the power of The Book of Mormon to deliver on these promises.

Learning the language of The Book of Mormon (and especially of 2 Nephi Chapters 12-24) will bless us with comprehension of a celestial vernacular that is soothing to our ears and calming to our souls. The voice of the Spirit can be rhythmical and melodious. As we hear it quietly whisper: "You're a stranger here," it is comforting for us to realize that we "have wandered from a more exalted sphere." (Eliza R. Snow).

The Book of Mormon was written so all the world might know that "every soul who belongs to the whole human family of Adam ... must stand to be judged of (his or her) works, whether they be good or evil." (Mormon 3:20). Everyone will be redeemed from spiritual death, to stand, at least briefly, in the presence of God at the Judgment Bar of Christ.

The Book of Mormon takes up its narrative in earnest in a land that was choice above all other lands, that was preserved so the children of God could flourish 'beyond the wall.'

It was
written and
preserved to come
forth in our day, so
that both the Jews and
and Gentiles might be
convinced that Jesus is
the Christ, the Son of
the Living God.

The Book of Mormon serves as another witness
to "the Jews, the covenant people of the Lord ... that
Jesus, whom they slew, was the very Christ and the very
God." (Mormon 3:21). As Nephi wrote, The Book of Mormon
will be given to the Jews in the Last Days "for the purpose of
convincing them of the true Messiah, who was rejected by
them; and unto the convincing of them that they need
not look forward any more for a Messiah to come ...
for there is save one Messiah spoken of by the
prophets, and that Messiah is he who
should be rejected of the Jews."
(2 Nephi 25:18).

Our Book of Mormon scholarship provides us with an attractive return on investment, and also with mad money that is sufficient for our immediate needs. But it also allows us, if we so choose, to substitute its legal tender for bundles of counterfeit currency with which late payments may be made with both interest and penalties tacked on for bad behavior. Without the Atonement, our lease on life would be threatened with cancellation for the nonpayment of the levies and the charges that accumulate as we conduct our lives within a speculative environment in an arena of agency and the circus of commerce.

Mormon saw our day and knew our needs. He understood that The Book of Mormon would help a world that did not know how to "repent, (to) prepare to stand before the judgment-seat of Christ. (Mormon 3:22).

"Men are free according to the flesh; and all things are given them which are expedient unto man. And they are free to choose liberty and eternal life, through the great Mediator of all men, or to choose captivity and death, according to the captivity and power of the devil; for he seeketh that all men might be miserable like unto himself."
(2 Nephi 2:27).

"And upon these I write the things of my soul, and many of the scriptures which are engraven upon the plates of brass. For my soul delighteth in the scriptures, and my heart pondereth them, and writeth them for the learning and the profit of my children. Behold, my soul delighteth in the things of the Lord; and my heart pondereth continually upon the things which I have seen and heard." (2 Nephi 4:15-16).

A Book of
Mormon requirement is
that we take calculated and
acceptable risks, in order to break
free from the comfort zones, safety
nets, and ports of refuge to which the
timid apprehensively retreat at the first
sign of danger, to squeak out their lives
as they scurry about from one shadowy
sanctuary to another, in a flight from
both freedom and faith.

It is
our faith that
points us in the
direction of doctrine,
so when we encounter
the principles of the Plan
in The Book of Mormon, we
will all experience religious
recognition, or a re-knowing
of things we have previously
been taught. We will respond
to the truth with action that
has the form and substance
of a godly walk that is a
bold testament of our
confidence in God's
power to save.

It took J.R.R. Tolkien 17 years to write "The Lord of The Rings." Margaret Mitchell took nearly 10 years to complete "Gone With The Wind." J.D. Salinger spent 10 years to complete "The Catcher in The Rye." It took Victor Hugo 12 years to complete "Les Misérables." Michael Crichton spent 8 years writing "Jurassic Park." It took Joseph Smith roughly 3 months to translate The Book of Mormon. How did he do it so quickly? He simply said that the task was accomplished "by the gift and power of God."

As we lift the latch and force the way, and we learn more about the Plan of God by studying The Book of Mormon, we begin to discern a distinct afterglow from the light of our premortal lives, that establishes a subtle but undeniable link between the heavens and the earth that remains undeniable.

The second
mile of faith that
is nurtured by the
Plan of God and by The
Book of Mormon asks us to
shun the telestial temptations
that are so cunningly peddled by
snake oil salesmen who have set up
shop within the great and spacious
buildings that dot the landscapes
of our lives, and that pop up in
the most unexpected places on
the side streets that border
the strait and narrow
way.

As we read and study The
Book of Mormon, we feel the word
enlarging our souls and enlightening
our understanding. As Brigham Young
said: "Every gospel principle carries within
it a witness that it is true." In the economy of
the gospel, "we often catch a spark from the
awakened memories of the immortal soul,
which lights up our whole being as with
the glory of our former home."
(Joseph F. Smith).

When we
feel the power of
The Book of Mormon
swelling within us, we
realize that it can lift us
to the zenith of experience,
until lines differentiating
mortality and eternity blur.
At that moment, when we see
ourselves in a condition that,
for the lack of better words,
can only be described as if
we were being born again,
we will be consumed in
fires of everlasting
burnings.

All of those
who have renounced
the world and have entered
into the Covenant "are born of
him." (Mosiah 5:7). Covenants are
binding contracts between ourselves
and God. Therefore, no person may enter
into such except upon the basis of revelation
from Him, and upon the exercise of priesthood
power by His appointed servants who have been
ordained to administer the ordinances of the
gospel. When these conditions have been
met, those in the embrace of fidelity
and fraternity with the Savior
are described as being
"born again."

Our temporal baggage is
one of the obvious contraries with which we
have to deal as we engage the grand themes of
the Plan of Salvation. It creates imbalance leading
to confusion, whereas the principles and doctrine of The
Book of Mormon jar us out of our collective complacency
by upsetting the stagnation of the status quo. They
invite us to enjoy a settled conviction of the truth
by getting our juices flowing, prodding us to
constructively expend our energy, and
putting our agency to work in the
best tradition of opposition
in all things.

As we study correct principles and
make determined efforts to incorporate
the teachings of The Book of Mormon into our
lives, we are obliged to return to the real world, where
we are resigned to be sent forth as sheep in the midst of
wolves. However, the efforts we have made to internalize its
principles and doctrines will create a shield of protection
against the spatter of corrosive perspiration cast off by
the destroyer, who is working overtime to damage
our doctrinal defenses, diminish our charitable
capacity, deplete our bountiful reservoirs
of empathy, dampen our spiritual
sensitivities, and destroy
our devotions.

Whether we are scions of society or practiced panhandlers, living in the fast or the slow lane of life, whether we have rags or riches, or are leaders or lepers, are early prodigies or late bloomers, venture capitalists or welfare recipients; no matter what our circumstances may be, The Book of Mormon is as a bridge over the troubled waters of faltering faith. When we embark upon its study, we move past the yellow brick road that leads only to Oz, to find the strait and narrow path that is cobbled with gold and that will take us to the gate of heaven itself.

When we are introduced to The Book of Mormon and our souls have been illuminated by the burning Spirit of God, we can no longer remain passive. The flickering fire of faith warms up our souls as we begin to recognize the upward reach within ourselves. We are sensitized to truth and beauty, and to a goodness above and beyond our own attainment. We experience the unmistakable stirrings of the Spirit from deep within our hearts.

Every one of the Book of Mormon prophets invites us to choose liberty and eternal life, rather than its contrary, which is captivity and spiritual death, and to live out our lives within the framework of the gospel and its laws. Without it, unbridled freedom would lead to tyranny. We are free to elect whether or not we wish to be governed by its principles and doctrines, but we cannot escape the consequences should we choose unwisely.

Those who share The Book of Mormon with others are faithful, and they endure, that they might obtain the prize of eternal life. They claim the promises of the Lord, Who said He would disperse the powers of darkness from before them, and would cause the heavens to shake for their good, as they go about the work of the ministry, bringing others into the fold.

Once we have embraced
The Book of Mormon, we speak
of principles with such incendiary
rhetoric that those who are of hesitant
and faltering faith are encouraged to
take their first tentative steps toward
commitment, while, simultaneously,
more spiritually mature disciples, as
they realize that present levels of
performance aren't acceptable,
are inspired to lengthen
their stride.

Paul knew
what it meant to go
the second mile. He labored
among the Corinthian Saints,
whom he was pleased to discover
had a working relationship with the
laws and ordinances of the gospel. He
characterized the revelatory gifts of God as
being written on 'tables of stone'. That is all
well and good, but he hinted that there exists yet
another order of mind. It is a connection that can
be ours if we will embrace The Book of Mormon.
"Ye are manifestly declared to be the epistle of
Christ ministered by us, written not with
ink, but with the Spirit of the living
God; not in tables of stone, but in
(the) fleshy tables of the heart."
(2 Corinthians 3:3).

We know that
God is sensitive to our
needs, because we have the
evidence of our effectual and
fervent prayers. We understand
the laws of heaven that govern the
acceptance by the world of The Book
of Mormon. We draw virtue from the
life force that is the Holy Ghost, and
encourage those who find themselves
lost in the press of the jostling crowd
to reach out and touch the hem of
the garment of the Savior.
(See Matthew 9:21).

When our hearts
have been touched by
the Spirit, and we begin
to grasp the nature of The
Book of Mormon and how it
was conceived, we learn more
about how we fit in to God's
divine design. We learn how
faith can drive the law into
our inward parts. When it
does so, the articles of
our faith become the
particles of our
faith.

We who have
experienced the power
of The Book of Mormon
will distain the amusement
parks of Babylon. Instead, we
will gratefully frequent the aid
stations that our Heavenly Father
has providentially positioned all
over Zion. We find our way by
avoiding telestial turf, and we
keep a sharp lookout for those
signposts that will lead us
to celestial boulevards
that are paved with
gold.

Those who have been
blessed with the capacity to
have wholeheartedly embraced
the principles and doctrines of The
Book of Mormon will find that they
have been endowed with an ability to
break free from "the influence of that
spirit which hath so strongly riveted
the creeds of the fathers, who have
inherited lies, upon the hearts of
the children, and filled the
world with confusion."
(D&C 123:7).

Those who have
so freely partaken of
the sustaining influence
of The Book of Mormon have
experienced God's power that
stems from love as opposed to
the Machiavellian influences
of lust and the unrighteous
desire for dominion that
dominate the agendas
of the worldly.

Is
it easier
to just throw
in the towel, and
harder to push on,
to continue the good
fight? Is it easy to settle
for average, and difficult
to be extraordinary? Those
who apprehend the philosophy
of The Book of Mormon accept
and will ultimately overcome
their challenges, not because
they are easy, but precisely
and pointedly because
they are hard.

The Book of
Mormon asks us to
emulate the protocols
of a criminal pathologist,
with one caveat. It seeks to
identify the fingerprints of
a master criminal, who is the
Prince of Darkness, which are
smeared all over a plethora of
penurious programs, parties,
politics, and policies that do
little else than to promote
personal and provincial
proclamations related
to plans that are, at
best, petty.

Too often,
the Nephites were
overzealous in their
outward observances. As
hypocrites, they pretended to
be pious, when, in fact, they were
simply professors of religion. They
crept into nameless graves, unwept,
unhonored, and unsung, while
now and then, a few of them
forgot themselves into
immortality.

It is in the pages of The Book of Mormon where we find the fulfilment, or a description of the realization, of many biblical prophecies. Without the clarification and illumination of its narrative, our understanding would be clouded by confusion, and we would see through a glass, darkly. (To name just a few examples, see 1 Nephi 13:12-15, 1 Nephi 13:16-19, 2 Nephi 2-27, Helaman 13-16, Genesis 49:22-26, Deuteronomy 33:13-16, Isaiah 29:1-2 & 18, Ezekiel 37:15-22, John 10:16, & 2 Corinthians 13:1).

The Savior's vicarious work of Atonement establishes a covenant relationship between ourselves and our Father that is equal in power and authority to any personal demonstration of obedience. Vicarious work is a key element of the Plan of Salvation.

The Book of Mormon
encourages us to feast upon
the word of Christ and ponder
the doctrines of the kingdom. We
receive God's strength to endure one
more day in righteousness. Our eyes
remain fixed upon the prize that is
the high calling of Jesus Christ,
and we taste the principles of
eternal life that are taught
with eloquence by its
inspired prophet-
historians.

Nephi explained that latter-
day Israel would need to learn the
things of the Jews, (see 2 Nephi 25:5),
to engage in a study of the scriptures that
reveals layers of meaning, until we reach the
point envisioned by the Dead Sea Covenanter,
who wrote: "For mine own part I have reached
the intervision, and through the spirit
thou hast placed within me, come
to know Thee, my God."
(11th Hymn).

From the dust, Nephi wrote of his preferred Hebrew poet: "Wherefore, hearken, O my people, which are of the house of Israel, and give ear unto my words; for because the words of Isaiah are not plain unto you, nevertheless, they are plain unto all those that are filled with the spirit of prophecy." (2 Nephi 25:4).

Obedience to principles that are elucidated in The Book of Mormon will release us from captivity and permit us to see things as they really are, and to enjoy a lucidity that stems more from our hearts, than from our heads.

The hallmark of Hebrew poetry is parallelism, which is the echoing of the thought of one line of verse in a second line that is its partner. This is called repetition of thought. Two lines of poetry are said to be parallel if the elements of one line correspond directly to those of the other, in a 1:1 relationship. For example; Lehi "was obedient unto the word of the Lord, wherefore, he did as the Lord commanded him." (1 Nephi 2:3).

There are many variations of parallelism in Hebrew poetry. One is a repetition of the same idea, which is called synonymous parallelism. ""Behold, I have dreamed a dream. Or, in other words, I have seen a vision." (Nephi 8:2). Another form illustrates a contrasting idea: "Wherefore, if a man have faith, he must needs have hope; for without faith there cannot be any hope." (Moroni 7:42). A third completes the idea of one line in a second line: "I am filled with charity, which is (God's) everlasting love." (Moroni 8:17).

Synthetic parallelism is a Hebraic literary device that ties together two related thoughts to emphasize behaviors, traits, or similarities, Rather than providing a 'contrast, or expressing the same idea in different words, as antithetical or synonymous parallelism would do, the second line of synthetic parallelism completes the thought of the first line. "Laban hath a record of the Jews and also, a genealogy of my forefathers, and they are engraven upon plates of brass." (1 Nephi 3:3).

In our busy and confusing world, we frequently see through a glass darkly. This makes it very difficult to discern, on our own, how to harness the tremendous power of the elusive equations that define the precise movement of a majestic clockwork that is found within the mathematics of The Book of Mormon. To accomplish that daunting task, we need the Holy Ghost to be our Tutor.

Climactic
parallel poetry
utilizes words that are
repeated in successive lines.
Additional information enlarges
the meaning until the climactic theme
that had been initiated in the first line is
completed. "The Lord knoweth all things from
the beginning; wherefore, he prepareth a way to
accomplish all his works among the children
of men; for behold, he hath all power unto
the fulfilling of all his words."
(1 Nephi 9:6).

Lastly,
there is a device that is
called a chiasm that repeats
line one, but in a reverse order.
If the second line is inverted, that
is to say, if its last element is placed
first, and the first, last, then a chiasm is
created, as in: "I will not put my trust in the
arm of flesh; for I know that cursed is he that
putteth his trust in the arm of flesh. Yea,
cursed is he that putteth his trust in
man, or maketh flesh his arm."
(2 Nephi 4:34).

The repetitive
pattern that is found
in Hebrew poetry illustrates
a spaciousness and dignity that
creates time for the thought to make an
impact on the hearer, and it also provides
an opportunity for the author to offer more
than one perspective. It is unselfconscious,
and remains remarkably free from the
artificialities of language that can
blur the meaning or intent of
many compositions.

Its structure, based as it
is on meaning, survives translation
with remarkably little loss, unlike poetry
that relies on a special vocabulary or a complex
meter. This is particularly significant when we
consider the remarkable fidelity of the translation
into the English language of the ancient records
that were delivered by Moroni into the hands
of the prophet Joseph Smith.

Hebrew poetry has the capacity
to plumb the depths of our own testimonies
by quietly turning our thoughts to our Creator,
reminding us that our God is in control, and that
by His divine design, those who love and serve Him
in righteousness and who obey the commandments
with exactness, will inherit the mansions that have
been prepared for them. It serenely bears witness of
the divine mission of our Savior. It illuminates
the path we must follow in order to receive the
blessings that are reserved for the faithful. It
teaches us about repentance, atonement,
and forgiveness, about His tender
mercies, and ultimately, about
the merciful Plan that He
has crafted for His
children.

As we immerse ourselves
in an earnest study of The Book
of Mormon, our investigation reveals
a polychromatic palate into which we
may dip the brush of understanding.
With God's gentle guidance, we may
paint broad strokes that capture not
only the addictive reverberations
of its delightful meter, but also
the enchanting detail of its
unanticipated beauty.

The poetic
nature of The
Book of Mormon
invites us to immerse
ourselves in the grandeur
of the world; to enjoy a greater
sense of all that's virtuous, lovely,
or of good report, and praiseworthy.
It reminds of the counsel of Nephi; to
press forward with complete dedication
and steadfastness, or confidence, with a
firm determination in Christ, having a
perfect brightness of hope, or faith, and
charity, which is the love of God and
of all men and women.

Opening The Book of
Mormon is like enjoying
our temple experience. We look
around ourselves in anticipation,
wondering what we might learn that
is new. Who will our teachers be today,
and how will the principles they desire to
convey be opened to our understanding?
How will the Holy Ghost touch us today?
Will we be inspired with insight, or will
it be intuition, inspiration, or perhaps
the dynamic energy of revelation
that will distill upon our minds
as the dews of heaven?

In light of the poetical beauty
of The Book of Mormon, the reality is
that many of those who continue to deny the
divine origin of that text must now admit that
even as they continue to cling to the belief that
its presentation is apocryphal, it remains a fine
example of an ancient "sacred" text that makes
a powerful statement in terms of its visions,
parables, poetry, and psalms, relating
to the worth of humanity in a world
where its merit is everywhere
questioned.

Book of Mormon
prophets reveal the Lord's
battle plan for the Last Days,
when His missionary army will
engage the forces of Babylon, whose
soldiers will die both temporally and
spiritually before the bombardment
of love unfeigned, the onslaught
of priesthood principles, and
the overwhelming clout
of covenants.

The phrase "and thus we see" is unique to The Book of Mormon; it is not found in any other book of scripture. Other related phrases that are also unique to that ancient text include "thus we see," "thus we may see," and "we can see," as well as "and thus we can plainly discern."

There are 2 other similar phrases in the Book of Mormon that are also found in other scriptures, but these phrases in the other scriptures don't convey the same significance as those in The Book of Mormon. The first is "we see," found in Alma 9:14, 12:24, 19:23 & 36, 26:37, 29:8, 37:26, 42:3, & 50:21, in Helaman 3:29, as well as in the Old Testament in Psalms 36:9 & 74:9, Jeremiah 5:12, and in the New Testament in John 9:41, Romans 8:25, 1 Corinthians 13:12, and in Hebrews 2:8 & 3:19.

The second is "we may see," that is found in 2 Nephi 15:9 and Helaman 12:2, and in the Bible in Isaiah 5:19, Mark 15:32 and in John 6:30. Other variations include "we saw" and "we shall see." A similar phrase that is unique to the Doctrine and Covenants is "and thus we saw," found in D&C 76:89, 91, & 92.

A related phrase, and one that was equally designed to capture the attention of the reader, is "that ye may learn." This can be found in Mosiah 2:17, Alma 32:12 & 38:9, and Mormon 9:31, and a broader application of the phrase "that ye may." can be found in Mosiah 2:21, 18:9 & 24:14, Alma 13:13, 32:12, 34:17, 37:6 & 38:12, 3 Nephi 11:13, 12:45, & 30:2, Ether 2:23, Moroni 7:16 & 10:7, to name just a few. These verses are not just doctrinal thoughts, but are warnings that were designed to help us to understand how relevant they are to our own circumstances.

For the Nephites, life consisted of an endless chain of spiritual experiences that were balanced by the constant counterpoint, or contrary, of worldliness. At first, one would think that there would be a wide gulf between the spiritual and the temporal, that would have made things easier for the righteous. These contrasting sides of human nature seem incompatible. But without a working knowledge of the principles governing opposition that are found in The Book of Mormon (see 2 Nephi Chapter 2) it would be much more difficult to reconcile the two and think of the Nephites as enjoying a state of holiness as their natural habitat, richer for having had their mortal experiences. They were not to be worn down by life, or to be overcome by evil influences, but rather were to be refined and purified by adversity, danger, misfortune, and challenges.

The Book of Mormon helps us to be quick to hearken to the words of the Lord. A Gospel Firearms Safety Course cautions us to never play with loaded weapons, for Satan stands like a sentinel, ready at any time to discharge his assault rifle in the direction of doctrine. Beelzebub's high velocity bullets of unbelief may harmlessly ricochet off the bedrock of well-grounded faith. However, they can be dangerous, and can even mortally wound the eternal identity of those who have not put on the whole armor of God. His explosive devices may be improvised, but they are insidious and insincere, incorrect, immoral, and impulsively disingenuous.

The Book of
Mormon helps us
discern the truths that
fueled Hamlet's euphoria:
"What a piece of work is man!
How noble in reason, how infinite
in faculty, in form and moving how
express and admirable, in action how
like an angel, in apprehension how
like a god - the beauty of the
world, the paragon of
animals!"

The Book of
Mormon is where we
turn for triage, when
we have been wounded by
the adversary's fiery darts.
It is our safe haven, where we
can firmly grasp the horns of
sanctuary and where our spirits
can be restored. Within its pages,
while we haven't as yet encroached
upon its sacred precincts, we can
still learn all about the order of
heaven, and how to honor the
sacred covenants that will
qualify us to live there
in a coming day.

Our eyes
become single
to the glory of God
when we catch the vision
of Book of Mormon study.
Over time, we will be converted
to its power, and our bodies will
be filled with light. There will be
no darkness in us, and we will
come to realize that it's withinq3
the realm of possibility to
comprehend all things.
(See D&C 88:67).

During our
study of The Book
of Mormon, we will surely
interact with members of the
church who grapple with their own
custom-tailored challenges, but who
through the grace of God have managed
to make the transition from hesitancy to
conviction, from instability to commitment,
from timidity to confidence, from indecision
to resolution, from doubts to certainty, from
struggle to celebration, and from vacillation
to purpose. In short, we will join the joyful
throngs who have made the transition
from spiritual itinerancy to
moral discipline.

With its
breathtaking reconciliation
of the Law of Justice with the Law
of Mercy, the doctrine of Atonement
within The Book of Mormon permits the
worst of us to work out our salvation with
fear and trembling before the Lord, as we
earn the privilege, us prodigal sons and
daughters of a Father Who loves us, to
rejoin His household of faith in full
fellowship, with all the privileges
one might hope for, subject to
the reformation of errant
behavior and flawed
character.

Within The Book
of Mormon, the fulness
of the gospel reassures us that
when the process of securing our
celestial legacy has been completed,
there will be no breaches in the shield
wall of our family history, there will be
no names missing from the book of life
that has been carefully compiled by the
angels in heaven, and there will be no
empty seats around the table, when
we all sit down together to enjoy
a reunion at family dinner
in our heavenly home.

It's been said
that time is a fire in
which we burn. This may
be true, in the sense that it is
by fire and the Holy Ghost that
time becomes an element we use
to work out our salvation with
fear and trembling before
the Lord, as we read The
Book of Mormon.

Possibly, the most
significant difference that
accounts for the superiority of the
principles of God's Plan of Salvation
that is revealed in The Book of Mormon
is the process whereby the gospel of Jesus
Christ is internalized by His disciples. The
wonder of our transformation begins with
sanctification by the Spirit at the waters
of baptism, and it only ends when we
have participated in the ordinances
of exaltation that are carried out
before holy altars in the
House of the Lord.

We read The
Book of Mormon
because our Lord of
Whom it testifies has
already accomplished
His exaltation, while we
clearly have yet to do so.
The pledges we make with
our Heavenly Father are as
stamps on our passports to
perfection. The promises in
Moroni 10:4-5 invite us to
clear customs with nothing
to declare but our testimony
of Jesus Christ. Emerging
into the light of day, there
will then be revealed before
us the rolling vista of an
undiscovered country-at
one and the same time
our destination and
our destiny.

After we have read and re-read The
Book of Mormon again and again, we
realize that the passage of time and growing
old with one of our favorite books of scripture is
simply a feature of mortality designed by God
as a brilliant mechanism that would afford us
the opportunity to gauge the approach of our
reunion with Him in the eternal world,
that will outlast time and will
endure throughout all
eternity.

In The Book
of Mormon, we learn
"how to give and not count
the cost, to fight and not heed
the wounds, to toil and not seek
for rest, and to labor and not ask
for reward, save that of knowing
that we do God's will."
(Loyola).

Nephi clearly
taught that, in the Last
Days, Satan would once again
raise the spectre of rebellion, and he
will "rage in the hearts of men, and stir
them up to anger against that which is good."
(2 Nephi 28:20). As the process of Restoration has
unfolded, he's fought a desperate battle to prevent the
receipt, translation, publication, and distribution of
The Book of Mormon. Having failed in those efforts,
he now struggles to substitute the sophistry of men
for the simplicity of the message. But that fraud is
all form and no substance, because it contributes
nothing to the welfare of Zion. Its driving force
seems to be a brazen craving for personal gain,
with a duplicitous message that is propelled
by a perceived power that is nothing more
substantive than the fleeting adoration
of an irrational world that, in its blind
fanaticism, has completely lost sight
of its objectives. His only option, it
would seem, is to hysterically
redouble his efforts in the
absence of a Plan.

We can be sure that the Lord will do "nothing save it be plain unto the children of men, and he inviteth them all to come unto him and partake of his goodness; and he denieth none that come unto him, black and white, bond and free, male and female; and he remembereth the heathen; and all are alike unto God, both Jew and Gentile."
(2 Nephi 26:33).

Joseph Fielding Smith taught that "every soul coming into this world came here with the promise that through obedience he or she would receive the blessings of salvation. No one has been foreordained to sin, or to perform a mission of evil."

"The Lord God worketh not in darkness (and) doeth not anything save it be for the benefit of the world; for he loveth the world, even that he layeth down his own life that he may draw all men unto him, Wherefore, he commandeth none that they shall not partake of his salvation." (2 Nephi 26:23-24). "For God so loved the world, that he gave his only begotten Son, that whosoever believeth in him should not perish, but have everlasting life." (John 3:16).

We are blessed to be able to live out our days of probation in the light of life that illuminates priesthood actions, ordinances, covenants, and prayers. These exercises strengthen our spiritual muscles and increase our capacity to stay spiritually aerobically fit, but they have meaning and purpose only because of God's grace, which blesses us to inhale deeply of a celestial ether that defies explanation and begs description. We are saved by grace, no matter what else we might have or do. Grace is a sine qua non, an essential condition for salvation, and the Saints, in particular, are blessed to be its grateful recipients.

"The ten thousand of my people ... were hewn down, being led in the front by me. And we also beheld the ten thousand of my people who were led by my son Moroni. And behold, the ten thousand of Gidgiddonah had fallen, and he also in the midst. And Lamah had fallen with his ten thousand; and Gilgal had fallen with his ten thousand; and Limhah had fallen with his ten thousand; and Jeneum had fallen with his ten thousand; and Cumenihah, and Moronihah, and Antionum, and Shiblom, and Shem, and Josh, had fallen with their ten thousand each." (130,000 in total). (Mormon 6:14).

The Central American Mexican chronicler, Ixtlilxochitl, reported of the Tultecas around 1,060 A.D. that in a three-year war, over five million were slain on both sides. Even allowing him considerable room for exaggeration, we are left with little doubt that the battle at Cumorah was within the realm of the plausible in Meso-American terms.

"The redeemed of the Lord shall return, and come with singing unto Zion; and everlasting joy and holiness shall be upon their heads; and they shall obtain gladness and joy; sorrow and mourning shall flee away." (2 Nephi 8:11). The Lord's promise is before the Latter-day Saints as both a challenge and an opportunity.

President Ezra Taft Benson taught that our church ecclesiastical units called the stakes of Zion have "at least four purposes. One is to unify and perfect the members who live within their boundaries, by extending to them the church programs, ordinances, and instructions. Secondly, the members of stakes are the models, or standards, of righteousness for the world. Third, stakes are to be a defense from the world. They do this as members unify under their local priesthood leaders and consecrate themselves to do their duty and keep their covenants. Fourth, stakes are a refuge from the storm that is to be poured out over the earth."

The Atonement, that is so
powerfully taught in The Book of Mormon, is
one of the tender mercies of the Lord and is the gold
standard of vicarious work. In our day, the Savior has
delegated authority to the members of His church to follow
His example, to act in behalf of the dead, of those who are
unable to perform saving ordinances for themselves,
since they have passed beyond the veil and are
living in the Spirit World while they
await the resurrection.

The Great Plan of Redemption (see Alma
34:31) required that "an Atonement should
be made. Therefore God Himself atoneth for the sins
of the world, to bring about the Plan of Mercy, to appease
the demands of Justice, that God might be a perfect, just God,
and a merciful God also." (Alma 42:15). Thru the Atonement,
God became the Master of the situation by placating Justice
while still mercifully reclaiming us from physical and
spiritual death. Through sacrifice, the debt would
be paid, redemption made, the covenant
fulfilled, Justice satisfied, His will
done, and all power given to
His Only Begotten
Son.

God's great Plan of
Restoration (Alma 41:2) is that
Adam fell that we might come to earth in
order to prepare for a resurrection. (See Alma
12:24). Through the Atonement of Christ, we
will be raised in the resurrection clothed in
immortality, in the kinds of bodies we
will need to dwell in the various
degrees of glory for which
we have qualified.

Our Father's Great Plan
of Salvation (see Alma 42:5) hinges
on baptism. Without it, we are doomed to suffer
in the shadows where we experience only illusions of
reality. Without obedience, the discrepancy between our
marginalized behavior and the ideals of the Plan become
so intense that our short-lived pleasure in worldly ways
must evaporate as the morning dew in the light of day.
When this disparity reaches "critical mass," a requisite
readjustment must tear down the façade of corruption
and hypocrisy to allow the cultivation of a more
nurturing lifestyle only made possible by the
Atonement of Jesus Christ, and related
obedience to the principles
of the Plan.

Alma taught the principles that relate to the Great Plan of Happiness. With no repentance, we would remain in a wretched state, and exist forever in our sins. (See Alma 12:26). Without baptism, if we were to partake of the fruit of the tree of life, which is eternal life, or the highest expression of the love of God, it would be impossible to sustain a celestial existence inasmuch as in our fallen condition we would be incapable of obedience to celestial principles. Thus, the Plan would be frustrated. Mercy and Justice were placed before Adam and Eve, to bar the way to the tree of life until they had the opportunity to participate in the saving ordinances of the gospel. (See Alma 12:21, 42:2, and Moses 4:31).

Alma taught that because of God's Plan of Mercy, (Alma 42:15), the principle of agency could be honored, allowing us to encounter opposition in a mortal setting and to gain experience, in spite of the fact that Justice would need to be served (in the absence of repentance and the Atonement) were we to violate eternal law in the process. When Jesus Christ stepped forward and offered Himself as the Lamb Slain From the Foundation of the World, the Plan swung into action, allowing us to die without jeopardizing our eternal glory, subject to our repentance.

Also by the author

Book of Mormon Commentary

- Volume One - Born In The Wilderness
- Volume Two - Voices From the Dust
- Volume Three - Journey to Cumorah

Compendium to Book of Mormon Commentary

- Volume One
- Volume Two
- Volume Three
- Volume Four
- Volume Five
- Volume Six
- Volume Seven
- Volume Eight

Book of Mormon Observations

- Volume One
- Volume Two
- Volume Three
- Volume Four

A Book of Mormon Commentary
Volumes One - Three

Compendia
Volumes One - Eight

Observations
Volumes One - Four

www.ingramcontent.com/pod-product-compliance
Lightning Source LLC
Chambersburg PA
CBHW061400010526
44107CB00012B/999